To my dear friend,
Dr. Paul Benjamin,
with appreciation for
the faithful witness
you gave.

[signature]
June 1973

The Reluctant Witness

The Reluctant Witness

Kenneth L. Chafin

BROADMAN PRESS
Nashville, Tennessee

ⓒ Copyright 1974 ● Broadman Press
All rights reserved
4255-50
ISBN: 0-8054-5550-7

Library of Congress Catalog Card Number: 74-84548
Dewey Decimal Classification: 248.5
Printed in the United States of America

Dedicated
to
my
father
and
mother

Acknowledgments

Acknowledgments are always inadequate, but I have this need to try to say thank you to the people who have had a part in this book.

It would be impossible to even list all the individuals who have stimulated and developed my interest in the potential of the laity. Dr. Elton Trueblood stands tall in this group. I began reading his books when I was a student and admired his commitment to the ordinary church member. I did my graduate thesis in the philosophy of religion on his apologetic method. Through the years, our lives have continued to cross. We've been on many programs together. I've spoken at the Yokefellow's Institute. He's been in my church and in my home. When he and Virginia were in our home the last time, he spent most of the time encouraging me to write some more. I love this man very much.

I owe much to the South Main Baptist Church, which had enough courage to call me to be its pastor even though I had been fifteen years in the classroom and working in evangelism in the denomination. The first fall I was in this distinguished pulpit I addressed myself to the challenge of communicating with effectiveness with modern man. That series of messages was the stimulus for writing the book. As you will discover, my perspective is not the study or the classroom but the congregation, where active people are trying to relate the gospel to their lives and the lives of others.

The process of proceeding from my "hunt and peck" draft of the manuscript to the well-styled book you hold in your hand leaves me in debt to many persons. The little Olympia portable on which I type doesn't spell well. And the Chicago manual of style has always been a mysterious book to me. Laura Mansfield took the first draft off tape. Connie Spencer did the final draft. Doris Estes, my secretary, and Barbara, my wife, worked with me on all the in-between stages which related to proofing, styling, correcting, and getting it to the publisher. Getting a book ready for the publisher is much like getting a child ready for college—there's a lot more involved than you had anticipated. And these were the people who went the second mile.

Mostly I want to thank that "army" called the people of God, the laity. It is really because of your interest and ability and commitment that I've written this book. I've talked to you and listened to you in a lot of different places across the years. And I hear you saying: "Help us. We have more to offer than we're giving and more potential than we're developing or using." If there's a paragraph somewhere in this book which God uses to "turn you on" to your own potential as a witness, then my efforts will be well repaid.

KENNETH CHAFIN

Contents

1
THE RELUCTANT
WITNESS
Acts 9:10-25

This book is written for those Christians who have not yet found a natural and satisfying way of sharing their faith in Jesus Christ. For just a little while, lay aside your frustrations. Turn away from your hang-ups and reactions. Forget the bad experiences you may have had. Walk with some of your brothers in Christ as they learn out of the uniqueness of their own experience to be used of God to point men to life eternal. It may be that the Holy Spirit will use their experience to make you more aware of your own potential.

Many of us are caught in a very uncomfortable trap when we begin to think about sharing our faith. On the one hand we live with a constant sense of *oughtness* about personal evangelism. We feel very much included in the command of Christ to "go into all the world and make disciples of all nations" (Matt. 28:19). Christ seems to be looking directly at us when he says, "you shall be my witness" (Acts 1:8). In addition to the scriptural commands to evangelize, we have an inner compulsion growing out of what we have experienced ourselves. This is heightened for us as we are constantly in contact with many people who seem to have no real meaning for their lives in this world—and no hope in the world to come.

On the other hand, we are often frustrated because we have not found a way to share our faith that is both natural and effective. After we have been motivated to witness, we are either left to work out our own technique of doing it or are shoved into some rigid, stereotyped, sterile approach which seems canned and unattractive. As a result of this, many genuine Christians with great potential give up on the possibility of becoming witnesses for Jesus Christ.

This book is about several very human individuals who found themselves a natural and effective way to share Jesus Christ with others. Each of these persons is different in his background, abilities, experiences, and opportunities—and these differences are reflected in how he witnesses. Somewhere in these pages perhaps you will meet a person with whom you can identify, and it could change your life!

The first person I want you to meet is named Ananias. He was one of the first Christians in the city of Damascus. Everything we know about him is recorded in fifteen short verses in the book of Acts (Acts 9:10-25). Yet in this one brief episode we find a person with whom practically every Christian can identify. The book of Acts begins with a great evangelistic service in which a sermon is preached and more than three thousand persons are converted. Since that time we have accepted the day of Pentecost as the norm for evangelism. This is unfortunate because our own experiences have not equipped us to identify with this. Except for the few individuals who happened to attend the Billy Graham Crusade in Korea where more than three thousand were converted in each service, most people do not identify personally with Acts 2.

But everyone can identify with Ananias because he is one person being sent by God to talk to another person. I have called him "The Reluctant Witness." As we understand his reluctance we may find a clue to our own foot-dragging. We should begin by reading carefully this brief account in Acts 9:10-25.

First, the Lord calls his name and he volunteers. We are often willing to obey before we get the instructions. "Here am I, Lord, send me," is easier to say if we don't know where he intends to send us. Abstract commitment is often easier than concrete obedience.

Next, God gave him specific instructions about the witnessing he was to do. Few people have had their prospect card filled out by the Lord himself. Ananias was told the street—Straight. He was told the name of the person and where he was staying—Saul of Tarsus, in the house of Judas. He was told in what circumstances he would find him—in a spirit of prayer and expectation. Most of us feel that if we had such assurances about our visiting, we would be anxious to go. Spectators always see things more clearly than the players, and if we had been Christians in Damascus at that time, we would probably have reacted exactly as Ananias did. Ananias did not want to go. God had to repeat and reinforce his command before he finally obeyed. Because he obeyed, all Christian history is different.

1. There are some valuable lessons to be learned from this experience for those of us who have been reluctant to share our faith. *The first lesson any Christian needs to learn is that fear is normal and can be controlled and used to great advantage.* A person must learn to deal realistically and redemptively with fear. This is an emotion experienced by every sensitive Christian who has considered sharing his faith. Ananias' first problem was that he was afraid. Any intelligent Christian of the first century would have been afraid of Saul of Tarsus. He was a zealous and successful persecutor of the Christians.

One night in a group studying the Bible, each of us was given a Bible verse describing one New Testament character. We were asked to tell how we would feel and act if that person lived next door. The person next to me had the verse, "Saul . . . entered house after house, seizing men and women, and sending them to prison" (Acts 8:3). My friend was asked to tell how he would go about witnessing to this neighbor. He thought a long time. Then very seriously he answered, "First, I would put all my things in order—then, I'd approach him very cautiously." Evidently, Ananias felt the same way. It is interesting, though, that it does not have to be a potentially dangerous person like Saul to make us afraid. It can be a loving relative, a gracious neighbor, a member of our club, an associate at work, a classmate at school, or even our own children.

For several years I was director of evangelism for my denomination. Working with some of the key leaders in the church, I spent more than two years deeply involved in developing a method of training laymen to share their faith. This involved an in-depth study and evaluation of all the different approaches being made by churches, denominations, and interdenominational groups. It involved listing some of the areas in which most laymen need specific help. The farther we got into the study, the more we realized that certain needs kept looming larger and larger: (1) The need for simple, basic Bible study that related to the meaning of repentance, faith, conversion, salvation, and the Christian life. (2) The need for spiritual growth. Most of the really exciting witnessing being done came out of a growth experience. (3) The need for some basic skills. This came as a surprise to many. It had been assumed that mature adults could naturally transfer the skills they had in other areas to that of witnessing. (4) The need for some practical experience under supervision.

It was this need which helped us to face the fear issue.

For many years we have been training people in evangelism with no immediate opportunity for putting what they learn into practice. The decision was made that on the fourth night of our training all the pupils would be divided into groups of threes and given assignments. They were to make three visits and give each person an opportunity to put into practice what he had been learning about listening, sharing, identifying with people, and inviting them to become Christians. Once it was understood that the whole emphasis of the school was to move from the theoretical to the intensely practical, the whole atmosphere changed. Suddenly there was tension. People began to drag out all their old hang-ups.

One of the first pilot schools of evangelism was held in a church in my neighborhood. It was understood from the beginning that we were all going visiting on Thursday night, but no one mentioned it. It became the hidden agenda for the week. The tension that built up was so real it could almost have been photographed. It was obvious by Wednesday night that many of those being trained were not planning to come on the night of the home visitation—and they didn't. As our staff and others evaluated this experience, the usual theories were advanced. One suggested that they weren't really Christians. Another felt the problem was commitment. A third felt that they needed more motivation. Finally, an honest and perceptive person put his finger on it: "They're scared!" It was decided that in succeeding schools we should bring into the open from the very first the matter of fear and deal with it.

In the next school the leader, Gil Stricklin, announced kiddingly on the first night: "On Thursday there are going to be two kinds of Christians—visiting Christians and chicken Christians." Everyone laughed and began to make the "cheep

. . . cheep . . . cheep" sound of a chicken. The surprise about
the experience was that *everybody* was scared. Everyone had
anxieties. Suddenly it began to dawn upon those present that
fear did not necessarily mean there was something wrong
spiritually. Fear was normal. Once fear was pulled from the
back of the mind into the open, it was possible to talk about
it, laugh about it, pray about it, and deal with it creatively.

Fear is natural because witnessing makes a person vulnerable. There is risk involved when you begin to share the
important experiences of your life and get into the sensitive
area of another person's life. This is why our natural tendency
is to try to keep the conversation on nonrisk subjects. We
can talk about church, weather, sports, Sunday School, children, and the weather without too much risk.

I was once stranded at the Atlanta airport for several hours.
To pass the time I went to the restaurant to eat a long leisurely
meal. Seated at the table next to me were four well-dressed,
well-educated, attractive young women. I could hardly believe
my ears when I overheard the subject of their conversation.
I became so interested that I timed them to see how long
they could keep it up. For forty minutes *they discussed cottage
cheese.* The one thing which could be said about the subject
was that it was safe. But before you are too critical of these
ladies, do a replay of some of your own conversations with
people. There is a lot of "cottage cheese" talk going around.
It is only when you move from the safe areas into talking
with people about what Jesus Christ has meant in your life
and what he can mean in theirs, that you open yourself up
and make yourself vulnerable.

Fear is natural because any genuine communication has
some unknown factors in it. I may have been a Christian
for years and I may have talked with many people before,
but each time I talk to another human being there is some-

thing unique about it. This is what makes life interesting. It would be pretty dull if everything were totally predictable. There is a certain intimidating aspect to wondering if you will be able to handle whatever comes up.

This is the fear which makes many people go to a style of witnessing that tries to eliminate the variations. There are some approaches to witnessing which suggest that you should be totally in charge by following a memorized approach which ignores whatever the other person says. Of course there are some funny and almost tragic things which can happen under these circumstances. At one time I was very critical of this approach. I still do not think it represents the best style of communicating. But I have come to believe that people have been drawn to it out of two reasons. First, the average person needs some method to organize his presentation. Second, this method takes away the fear of the uniqueness of each situation by ignoring it.

However, there is a better way to deal with this fear. First, the Christian should rejoice that each encounter with other human beings is different. This keeps communicating from becoming "old hat." If every one looked alike, thought alike, talked alike, and responded in the same way, then the work of evangelism would get as dull and monotonous as work on an assembly line where every day was the same. Second, the unique nature of each situation keeps the Christian from trying to be "Mr. Know-Everything." Instead it helps him to focus on sharing what he does know.

Often we are afraid because of the way we feel people are apt to react to us. We have some preconceived notions about how people will treat us if we start to verbalize our faith. Most of this is just in our minds. The overwhelming experience of those who regularly talk to other people about Jesus Christ is that they are treated politely and with interest.

There will always be a few exceptions—people who will be rude or thoughtless—but they will not be the rule. In literally hundreds of first-time efforts by Christians to witness, the reports of how they were received were overwhelmingly positive. They said things like: "They thanked me," "They didn't want to me to leave," "They invited me back."

Sometimes fear is born of an erroneous idea of what success is. A successful witness is a person who in love and in the power of the Spirit shares Jesus Christ and then leaves the results to God. Any time we go into a situation feeling that we have failed unless we get a certain commitment or response out of the person we witness to, we will always have fear. Because of this false standard of success we will be apt to pressure people who are not ready or seek commitments from individuals who do not understand. Once our ego is no longer a factor in the success, we can relax and let God use us in a more effective way.

Fear can be controlled. Developing certain skills can help. We can learn to relate to people. We can learn to listen and be sensitive to others. We can learn to share our own story in such a way that it has meaning for others. We can actually learn to invite people to Jesus Christ. As we mature and become more experienced, all of these factors will help us to keep fear under control rather than let it control us.

Fear is normal. It can be controlled. It can also be useful. Fear will cause us to pray more. It will make us more realistic about our dependence upon God and our partnership with him. It will motivate us to develop those skills and understandings which improve our abilities. It will introduce into our witnessing a healthy tension, which is a part of all important communication. Once fear is accepted as normal, it can become a servant that can be used redemptively.

2. *The second lesson the reluctant witness must learn is that*

God is already at work in the lives of those to whom he is sending us. This is a valuable lesson, but one that is difficult to learn. In the Scripture passage we read, Ananias thought that God was working only with him but not with Saul. Ananias did not want to be the first contact with this dangerous person. Who could fail to identify with Ananias' anxiety? Yet he really had no reason to be anxious because God had already been at work in the life of the man to whom he was sending him and was already preparing Saul's heart for the gospel.

For too long God's people have failed to realize that he is already at work in the lives of the people to whom he sends us. We are not being sent out to a hostile world into which God has not gone. We are invited to *follow* him into his world and bear witness. This means that we will never encounter a person whom God does not love. We will find some we do not love, or that others do not love, or even people who do not love themselves. But we will never meet a person God does not love. This means we will not meet a person who would not be better off if they followed Christ. This means that we will not come to a person that the Holy Spirit of God has not dealt with in some way. For Ananias the reluctance ceased when he realized he could say to Saul, "The Lord *who appeared to you* sent me" (Acts 9:17). This is a marvelous statement because it recognizes that God is always at work at both ends.

It has always been hard for us as God's children to realize that his compassion is broader than our narrow interests. Remember when God came to the apostle Peter at the house of Simon the tanner in Joppa. God had also been at work in the experience of a Roman Centurion named Cornelius from Caesarea when he wanted Peter to go witness. Peter was reluctant to go because he found it hard to believe that

God had any work that the leaders of the church had not authorized. All of us need to learn that the compassion and work of God is not limited to the people we have enrolled in our Sunday School, or to the circle of our friends, or to the list of people who seem interested.

We are living in a day when there seems to be a moving of the Spirit of God in the lives of many people. There is more openness to the gospel of Jesus Christ than there has been in years. The Spirit seems to be using many things to prepare the hearts of men. Many of the alternatives to Jesus Christ which seemed so attractive a decade ago have turned out to be dead-end streets. The very pace of life, with its unprecedented change, is ripping up the lives of people. All of these events seem to be plowing up the souls of men preparing them for the gospel. I am convinced that God has more people ready to receive the gospel than he has people ready to share it.

But we should not kid ourselves into believing that the spiritual hunger of modern man will make him look up "church" in the yellow pages and call for help. Modern man often does not label his emptiness as a spiritual hunger. Many never even think of "church" and "Christ" in their search. This is why they are so vulnerable to every sort of false hope. Consequently, they start buying astrology charts, reading Zen, or going to a Reader. These approaches do not have the answer—they only testify to how earnest the search is.

My first dramatic lesson as to how God is at work in the lives of people came while I was still a seminary student. I had just finished a course in evangelism. In the class we had memorized pages of Bible verses to be used as answers to the problems we would encounter when we began to talk to people. I had dozens of verses to answer such expected statements as "The church is full of hypocrites" or "I'm not sure the Bible is true." Having finished the class, I was invited by an old college buddy to conduct a meeting in a little rural church in eastern New Mexico. They had no pastor, and my friend who was the Sunday School director decided that each day we would visit in the homes of people who had attended who were not Christians. On the way to visit the first couple, I found myself reviewing all the verses I had memorized as answers to the objections I was sure I was going to get. We went in and sat down. The man asked my friend what we were there for. To my horror my friend, without any preliminaries, said, "I've brought Kenneth down here to talk to you about becoming a Christian." To my surprise the man said: "I'm glad. My wife and I have been talking about our need to become Christians." Within minutes the two of them had made a personal commitment of themselves to Jesus Christ. God had taught me that he goes ahead of his children to prepare the way.

Several years ago I helped train some wonderful laymen in a church in Honolulu. All week long as we talked about the spiritual needs of our friends and of God's love for them, they kept reminding me that the situation in Honolulu was different because of the Oriental culture. It was interesting to listen to the excited people when they came back from visiting and sharing in the homes. They were greatly surprised that "it was as though the Lord had gone before them." Our reluctance will fade away if we will but realize that we do not go alone.

3. *The third lesson that the reluctant witness needs to learn is that God has plans for the lives of those to whom we go.* God had to remind Ananias that "this man is my chosen instrument to bring my name before the nations and their kings" before he would go. (See Acts 9:15.) Little could Ananias have anticipated that this was the man whom God

would use to pen almost half of the books in the New Testament and to be the chief witness to the Gentile world. To Ananias, Saul looked like trouble. To God he looked like a messenger to the nations. The world is full of people that we've given up on for whom God still has great plans.

The teacher who looks out on a group of squirming boys and girls has no idea what God will someday accomplish through them. When we look at some of the men who have had such profound influence upon the world, we cannot help but wonder what might have happened had their lives been touched by an effective witness. Both Marx and Lenin lived for long periods of time, during their impressionable years, within walking distance of many Christians. We do not know but that the leaders of the movements of tomorrow, for good or bad, are living within the sphere of our influence now. When a child is taught the Bible, when a student is won to Christ, when a young married couple is introduced to Jesus, God is given an opportunity to work his plan for the world through them. Many of us are like Ananias. What we do for God may not be great. But it is possible that God will use someone to whom we witness to make all the difference in this world.

I can identify with anyone who is reluctant to take up a large and costly responsibility. But I also know that I must listen again to God's command and must obey. My fear can be controlled. God has gone ahead. He has plans for the people with whom I share.

2
THE INTRODUCER
John 1:40-42

It is a shame that Homer Covey and Andrew could not have gotten acquainted. They had a lot in common, especially their style of witnessing. Once a Christian comes to the conclusion that God wants to bear a witness through him, he needs to begin seeking the way. There are many who can identify with the reluctance of Ananias, but who are not quite ready to go down to "the street called Straight" to talk to someone. Let me introduce you to Andrew. I'll tell you about Homer Covey later.

Andrew is not known as a great orator, or as a great theologian, or as a great preacher, or as a great organizer, or as a great administrator. He is remembered mainly because he specialized in introducing people to Jesus. It didn't seem like much, but every time we come across him in the Gospel of John, he is introducing people to Jesus. If the centuries would be kind to you and me, it would be good to be known as individuals who introduced people to Jesus.

While Andrew was an apostle, unlike his brother he was not a part of the inner circle. This would bother some people. It would ruin their relationship with the church. He wasn't the chairman of the deacons. He probably wasn't even a deacon. He was not an officer in the church who reported

on business meeting night. He was not a chairman of one
of the key committees of the church. He just somehow never
found himself in the center where the power was. It was
always his brother, Simon Peter, and James and John that
Jesus called aside to share very intimate and precious moments with him.

Even worse, wherever Andrew is referred to in the Bible,
he is identified as Simon Peter's brother. Most of us like
to be known by who *we* are, not whose relative. Even the
text which tells that he was the one who led Peter to Christ,
starts out by saying, "Andrew, Simon Peter's brother" (John
1:40). I experienced this the day I got married. Barbara and
I were married in south Georgia where she was reared and
where she was greatly loved, where she had gone to school,
and where she had worked in some of the churches. Scores
of people came by and told me how fortunate I was to get
the finest young woman who had ever come out of that
church. I knew then that in south Georgia I was going to
be "Barbara Burke's husband." I've got a feeling that Andrew
must have gotten tired at times of being known as Simon
Peter's brother. I think every one of us has probably suffered
from being identified only by a relationship to somebody
else. The interesting thing about Andrew was that it didn't
seem to bother him. It may have been a thing that he had
to get a little help from God with, but there is a kind of
selflessness in this man that I would like to have.

And I wonder if he didn't get the clue for his personality
from the selflessness and example of John the Baptist. Andrew was first a disciple of John the Baptist. When the
tensions began between the disciples of Jesus and the followers of John the Baptist, Andrew was there. He may have
listened to John the Baptist's reply when his disciples began
to worry that Jesus was now baptizing more than they were.

Do you remember his statement, "He must increase but I must decrease"? (John 3:30, KJV). It would be so good for this spirit to permeate the whole life of the church. Then every petty rivalry could be laid aside.

And do you remember when Jesus came to be baptized, John said, "Behold the Lamb of God that takes away the sins of the world"? (John 1:29). And four of John's best disciples went with Jesus. It may be in the spirit of John the Baptist that Andrew had learned something. James and John didn't. Their mother was always trying to see which one of them was going to sit at the best seat in the kingdom of God. There was always a nagging ambition with others, but somehow it didn't bother Andrew.

People like Andrew are the real heroes of the faith. A church has *one* pastor but *many* members. And I'm wondering if when we come to the end of time we're not going to discover that the significant gains have been brought about by the "Andrews." People that were not prominent. People that we did not hear much about. People who did not give a lot of credit to themselves. But people who essentially made a vocation of introducing people to Jesus Christ.

Let's look at three episodes in Andrew's life. The first one is from John 1:40-42. I think you'd be interested to know that although Andrew is mentioned in Mark and in Matthew, all of these accounts are in John. John, in attempting to interpret the meaning of Christ's coming, felt these incidents were crucial to our understanding.

First is the story of his own conversion and the winning of his brother to Christ. "One of the two who heard John speak, and followed him was Andrew, Simon Peter's brother. He first found his brother Simon, and said to him, 'We have found the Messiah' (which means Christ). He brought him to Jesus. Jesus looked at him and said, 'So you are Simon the son of John? You shall be called Cephas' (which means Peter)' " (John 1:40-42).

This is an interesting account. Simon and Andrew lived together. We know that when Jesus went to their home and healed Peter's mother-in-law they were all there. But we also get from this picture that they both were disciples of John; they were both seekers after the Messiah. It was a very natural thing for them to share what they had found.

Evangelism *does* begin at home. This is probably the most needed place. But this is also often the most difficult place. I went through a period in my life when I felt that the easiest people to bear witness to ought to be your relatives. I was in for some bitter disappointments. I had some cousins and aunts and uncles who were not Christians, and I think when they saw me coming they must have just dreaded my getting there, because it was "old witnessing Ken." I probably created a lot of negative feelings about God by trying to witness the wrong way. What is it that makes it so difficult to bear a witness to your relatives? The closeness is a part of the problem. To your brother or to your sister, to your mother or to your father, or to an aunt or to an uncle, you are naturally very close. They often feel your talking to them is a violation or betrayal of that trust.

Also, we often get so emotionally involved in our witness to people we love that the intensity comes through, but the love does not. I have seen a wife or a husband or a teenager scar and hurt someone they loved by the way they tried to witness to them.

The most difficult witness I ever bore in my life was to my father. I was twenty-five years old and he was forty-five. I had been a Baptist preacher for several years. My father was living in Kansas and came to spend a week with me when I was preaching in a little church in northeastern Oklahoma.

All week long I prayed for God to deal with my father. I prayed and prayed and I preached and preached, and he just sat there. Finally, I decided that I would have to talk to my father. Now if you had asked me to go talk to *your* father, I could have done it easily. But every time I would open my mouth to try to talk to my father about Jesus, all I could think of was the things I had done that had hurt my father. And so finally I just said, "Dad, I want you to know that I'm terribly sorry for anything that I've ever done to hurt you." That was as far as I got. I started crying. I never did get to talk to him about becoming a Christian. But that night my father committed his life to Jesus Christ. It was the most difficult thing I ever tried in my whole life. And that's why I have such great admiration for a person like Andrew for whom it was so natural and so easy to reach out and to share with his brother.

A second episode in the life of "The Introducer" is found in John 6:8-9. It is a marvelous little story. You are already very familiar with it. Jesus has been preaching to a multitude. They've stayed through a couple of mealtimes and they're hungry, and some of them are fainting. One of the disciples announced that they didn't have enough money to buy food. Jesus has them look around. "One of his disciples, Andrew, Simon Peter's brother, said to him, 'There is a lad here who has five barley loaves and two fish; but what are they among so many?' " (John 6:8-9). You know the rest of the story. This is an interesting experience. I've asked myself why the author of John would put this one little insignificant statement here made by Andrew. And I came to the conclusion that it *wasn't* an insignificant statement.

Here is a person who is sensitive to the gifts people have which need to belong to Jesus Christ. One of our members has thrilled me as he has described for me some of the people in this town. And occasionally, after having introduced me to people, he has said to me privately: "This fellow's life is so mixed up, but he has so much to offer to God. I just wish he could become a Christian. I wish God could get a hold of his life. God needs what he has." You and I need to look around. Instead of looking around at people who are likely to become followers, maybe we ought to become sensitive to people who have gifts which God desperately needs.

A third episode in the life of "The Introducer" takes place during the last week of our Lord's earthly ministry. "Now among those who went up to worship at the feast were some Greeks. So these came to Philip who was from Bethsaida in Galilee, and said to him, 'Sir, we wish to see Jesus.' Philip went and told Andrew; Andrew went with Philip and they told Jesus" (John 12:20-22). This is a story of Jesus that took place probably in the Court of the Gentiles at the Temple in Jerusalem. On Tuesday afternoon in that last week things were very tense. The Pharisees were looking hard to find anything with which to accuse him. The story shows Andrew again so natural in this role of "The Introducer."

Is it possible for you and me as serious followers of Jesus Christ to develop a style of introducing people to Jesus? Many times I have gone to somebody's house and they have taken me by the hand and said, "I've got someone here I want you to meet." Is it possible for a person living in today's world to develop a style of introducing people to Jesus that is natural and effective? Many have done just that, and each in his own unique way reflecting his own gifts. Let me share a few ways, not necessarily to be copied, but to be used as a catalyst for your imagination. Adapt one of these or create a way all your own.

1. *Your home could be your base of operations for introducing people to Jesus Christ.* I once saw a lady in Richmond, Virginia. Everyone kept saying to me, "She is such an entertainer." I kept wondering whether she sang or played the piano. Then I discovered what they meant. She had made an art of bringing people to her home that she wanted to introduce to Jesus Christ. She did it subtly. She never made speeches. She just invited others who knew Jesus Christ and let a social occasion become the basis for a natural sharing. Through the years many people who have become followers of Jesus first became interested because of the warmth they felt as she entertained in her home.

When the Bill O'Brien's went to Indonesia as missionaries, they made their home their most effective tool for witnessing. Instead of a chapel or a clinic or an office, they used their home. They bought a beautiful home in a nice section of the city, one in which entertaining was easy. Then they made every conceivable event an occasion for inviting friends and neighbors into their home. They celebrated birthdays, anniversaries, holidays, and every possible event both American and Indonesian. These occasions became an opportunity to share something special in their lives. Many people of every station and class in Indonesia were introduced to Jesus Christ in their home.

There are some of you who have beautiful homes. And you have many friends who do not know Jesus Christ and the wholeness he brings. There are people who would come to your home for an enjoyable evening that you could never bring first to your church. Is it possible that God has put you where you are to make you an introducer of people to Jesus Christ?

2. *A person can use his social life to become an introducer.* Nothing is more attractive to me than watching the members

of my church enjoy doing things together. One who knows Christ should have a joy in living that manifests itself in all the areas of his life, especially his social life. As I have watched these friends play together, travel together, attend athletic events together, I have marveled at the quality of the friendships which have developed and the sheer joy they have in living. The average non-Christian does not know that such a relationship between people exists anywhere in the world. Could a person introduce people to Jesus Christ by introducing them to this fellowship?

I know I'm suggesting something to you that could be a little intimidating. One of the wonderful things about friends is that you finally learn about each other and you don't have to start over. There's always a risk in opening up any relationship. But isn't that what life is all about? And isn't the Dead Sea known mainly for receiving and not putting out? And isn't there a possibility that somehow in sharing in our social life as Christians, it might be a method by which we could introduce people to Jesus Christ?

3. *Sharing Christian friends is probably the easiest method.* I have occasionally been with people, and they didn't tell me why, but they included some people who ordinarily were not a part of their "traffic pattern." Occasionally they'll tell me afterwards: "Well, I wanted him to meet you because he's had sort of a bad experience with preachers. He doesn't think they are real people. I didn't want to tell you ahead of time because I just wanted you to be yourself." This is a part of a strategy. And quite frankly, it is a very effective strategy. With your children, the people you have in your home sometimes represent the finest witness that you can bear to them. Sometimes children are more fascinated with people who come into their home as visitors than with anyone else. I've watched my own children respond to guests. I

remember my own response to people who came into our home. Sharing Christian friends is a method of introducing people to Christ.

4. *It is possible to introduce people by sharing Christian events.* When I was a seminary student in Fort Worth, Texas, there was in the Broadway Baptist Church a man named Homer Covey. He had been president of the Chamber of Commerce. He was president of Worth Foods, a chain of grocery stores in the city. When Homer Covey was about sixty-five years old, H. Guy Moore led him to faith in Jesus Christ, and he became a radiant Christian.

Now, in spite of the fact that Homer Covey had run the Chamber of Commerce and was the president of a corporation, he was timid about articulating his faith. I don't think *that* is uncommon. I think there are people who can run vast corporations who are nervous about talking to one person about Jesus Christ. So he devised himself a plan. He began to pick out friends that he felt needed to experience what had happened to him. And then he began to look around for something that was going on that his friend would be interested in. He invited friends to the men's meeting. Some he invited to his Bible study class. Others he invited to hear his pastor speak. He became a specialist at sharing Christian events with his lost friends.

A very simple strategy, wouldn't you think? Yet when Homer Covey died, he left a score of men in Fort Worth who had become Christians because in his own way he had become an Andrew. He had become an introducer of men to Jesus Christ.

Are you beginning to see the amazing possibilities for those who really want to introduce people to Jesus Christ? The only limitation is our imagination and commitment. Make a list of all the people you know and are in contact with who need desperately to know God and the life he can bring. Is there a possibility that God might want to use you to introduce them to Jesus Christ? Maybe you and Homer Covey and Andrew could have this one thing in common. You could be known as the people who "always had someone you wanted them to meet."

3
LEARN TO TELL YOUR STORY

Acts 22:3-16

The first time I went to Laity Lodge, Keith Miller was the director. It was a great experience for me. After the meal on the first night Keith announced that a couple from Corpus Christi was going to give their testimony. For some reason, I was not quite able to understand why, I didn't look forward to it at all. It was a mistake on my part, because when they got up God really spoke through them to me and everyone there. All they did was tell about themselves—how they had met and married, how they had been reared in the church but without any real interest, and the events which led them to a vital faith and changes in their lives. It was humorous. It was emotional. It was moving. It was honest. It was so easy to identify with. It was believable. It made everyone think, That's what needs to happen in my life.

Afterwards in my room, I tried to analyze why I at first had reacted so negatively toward the whole idea of a testimony. I remembered attending little schoolhouse meetings with my mother as a child and listening to the "testimony time." After the group had sung for a while, the leader would ask for testimonies from the audience. The thing I remembered was that everyone who stood said essentially the same thing. The testimony had become so stylized that they all sounded alike—canned, memorized, and lifeless.

My experience at Laity Lodge, and countless experiences since then, has led me to believe that every child of God has a story to share. It represents one of the finest tools the Holy Spirit can use in helping others to know Jesus Christ. It may be that you are one of those persons who needs to quit being nervous about the testimony and learn how to use it to help others. I went back to my classes at the seminary determined to help my students articulate in a natural and believable way the story of what God had done in their lives.

The idea of a personal testimony did not originate with the twentieth-century renewal movement. The New Testament is filled with accounts of individuals sharing what God has done for them. But in all of the Bible none so consistently used his testimony as a tool in witnessing as did the apostle Paul. Luke records it several times, probably because he heard it more often than anything else. Paul used every connection he had to get a hearing for Jesus Christ. It might be his Roman citizenship, his knowledge of Greek or Hebrew, his training as a rabbi, or some experience he had. But in all these circumstances the story he told was his own experience. God used it to gain a beachhead in a pagan world.

The account used as a backdrop to this study is recorded in Acts 22:3-16. Paul had been seized by a mob and dragged from the Temple. He was rescued from the mob by soldiers who stopped the beating but nevertheless shackled him with chains. When the captain was unable to find out Paul's identity or offense from the crowd, he took him to the barracks. As they were entering, Paul spoke to the captain in Greek and asked for permission to speak to the people. He was impressed and granted his request. Paul stood and addressed the Jews in Hebrew. Take a few moments to reread the testimony he gave. It is direct and personal. It is detailed and believable. It is moving and searching. It is a classic example of a Christian telling his own story.

There are many reasons why a Christian ought to learn to use his own experiences in witnessing. (1) *First, people identify with a testimony.* This is why advertising agencies never tire of using them. This is why biographies are usually more interesting than essays. This is why the average person remembers the illustrations in a message longer than the definitions.

I remember that on Christmas our church observed Student Night at Christmas. The pastor invited several members who were away in college to give testimonies. I particularly remember two girls who were on the program. The first one stood and gave a beautifully prepared and well-delivered speech. It would have gotten a high grade in any speech class. You could see people smiling their approval and making a mental note to put her on that list of people who are called on to "give devotionals."

The second girl was obviously a bit shaken by having to follow so polished a performance, but she had no reason to be. She said: "I must have misread the pastor's instruction. I didn't know I was to give a speech. I just want to tell you of a wonderful experience I had learning to pray as a freshman in college." The increased interest was obvious. Because, while the first girl had shared a speech, this girl was going to share something of herself.

When we begin to open up to others and share with them out of our own lives, it becomes easier for them to share with us. Communication is a two-way affair. There's talking *and* listening. There is learning and sharing. We need both a radar for being sensitive to others and a microphone for sharing. I've noticed that it is easier for me to share with a person who has shared with me.

(2) *The personal testimony has authority in it.* One of the problems felt by the beginning witness is that he knows so little about the Bible. He knows so little church history and so little doctrine that he wonders if it isn't a mistake to try to share with others. This is one reason the testimony is a good place to begin. It is the place where *you* are the authority. It is the telling of your story.

It is important to study and understand the Bible. It is an important tool in witnessing. (Later in the book we will be learning how to use it better.) I have been a minister for more than twenty-five years. In addition to attending a seminary I taught in two of our schools for eleven years. In spite of all this study and experience, I still find myself talking to people about Jesus Christ and being asked questions that I have to answer with, "I don't know." But that doesn't stop me, because there are some things I *do* know, and that's what I'm sharing.

John's Gospel records a priceless story of a man born blind whom Jesus healed (John 9:1-38). The story begins with our Lord's unwillingness to get involved in a discussion of "why" the man was born blind. Then Jesus makes a salve from saliva and dust and spreads it on the man's eyes with instruction to wash them in the nearby pool of Siloam.

The man's sight came to him and great excitement followed. But the religious leaders were so bogged down in petty rules that they could not rejoice with the man's good fortune. They were upset that the healing had taken place on the sabbath. They confronted the man's parents, but they were afraid to commit themselves. So the leaders went to the man whose sight had been restored and put great pressure upon him to make some statement about whether Jesus was a sinner for having violated the sabbath.

The man's answer is a classic and should serve as a model

for all of us when we are confronted with areas in which
we are not experts. Listen to this powerful statement made
by an ignorant man under pressure in the presence of the
most learned: "Whether or not he is a sinner, I do not know,"
the man replied. "All I know is this: once I was blind, now
I can see" (John 9:25).

(3) *The personal testimony can be used in many different
situations.* Life does not organize itself into formal opportunities to witness. It would be nice if we could anticipate those
times when we would be called to "testify" and could put
on our "witnessing hat." However, the lives we live are lived
in many places. The witness we give verbally must be given
in the context of life. This life is lived in the context of rearing
our children, of getting acquainted with neighbors, of working
in myriad organizations for business and pleasure. In these
situations there are moments of seriousness in which a person
is able to express his own feelings and experiences. There
are times when the most natural thing to do is to share your
own experience.

Some of the most eloquent witnesses ever given have been
"one liners," shared in the context of life at a moment of
great need. The people we are around get frustrated with
their jobs and sometimes with themselves. They make mistakes. Their parents die. Their children get them down. They
get sick and discouraged. In the context of all these experiences which make up life, often a loving word of witness
and encouragement is what God uses to open a life up to
his wonderful love.

Every Christian has something worth sharing. I know exactly what many of you are thinking. You think that because
you did not have a "Damascus Road" experience that you
really do not have anything worth sharing. You couldn't be
more wrong. It is true that there are people who have had

striking experiences and are gifted in telling their story to large audiences with effectiveness.

I can understand the emotion of the man who went to hear an evangelist who had been converted from a life of underworld crime. That night in his prayers he said to God: "Oh, Lord, I've never smoked pot, been drunk, committed adultery, robbed a bank, or lied to a grand jury, but if you can use me in spite of these shortcomings, I want to be used!" We all need to realize that for every "Paul" converted on the road to Damascus there are thousands of "Timothys" who come to know Christ in a quiet way as the result of the witness of faithful parents and grandparents. While the striking testimony makes good programming, it is the more ordinary experience which is easier to identify with.

Many sensitive Christians feel a certain guilt in talking about what Christ is doing in their lives because they still have so many areas in which they have needs. I'm afraid that some of this attitude about "witnessing out of perfection" has been created by those of us who stand in the pulpits and seem to suggest that the decision to follow Christ solves all of your problems. While it is true that turning your life over to Jesus Christ brings forgiveness of sin and eternal life, it is equally true that this new allegiance and this new direction creates new tensions and new frustrations and new problems. The person who is floating along in this world giving in to every impulse will have some problems with guilt. The person who turns from sin to God for forgiveness will still have problems with temptation.

It does not ring true when a person says, "I'm so glad that Christ is my Savior. I committed my life to him when I was nine years old and have been completely happy ever since." Becoming a Christian does not take you out of your body with its accompanying impulses, out of this world with all its pressures—nor does it exempt you from the frustrations of adolescence. The sooner a Christian becomes aware that this is the world in which all men live and the arena in which Christ and the church are being helpful to us, the sooner he will cease being reluctant to witness because he is not yet a "saint."

I taught the Bible at one of Howard Butt's Laymen's Leadership Institutes recently. One of the outstanding features of each session was a witness by an individual or a couple. The one witness which captivated almost everyone was given by a housewife/mother who not only told how she came to know Christ but shared with honesty how frustrating it can sometimes be trying to cope with self-willed, noisy, healthy children. Had she been a bit more pious she probably would not have told of the morning she finally reached the breaking point and went around crunching everyone's cereal with her hands. But she told us, and we laughed and saw ourselves in it. It took nothing from her testimony for us to discover that she was a human being. She was real, and God used her.

The first person I ever heard articulate the idea of bearing a witness out of one's weakness was my wonderful friend Keith Miller. While there are some who have gone too far and have become exhibitionists, the point is still valid. The Christian who has all the answers and cruises around hunting someone to drop them on will discover that people avoid him like a plague. But the very real human being who has found in Christ the capacity to accept his own humanness will find a constant line of people wanting to tell their situation and ask if God has any hope or help for them.

Every Christian, whatever his personality, has something to share which God will use to help people. One of the terrible stereotypes many have about witnessing is that it is for the loud, aggressive, extroverted, "Mr. Personality" types.

Dr. James Kennedy is the pastor of the Coral Ridge Presbyterian Church in Ft. Lauderdale, Florida. He, more than any one minister in America, has come to symbolize the training of the laity to share their faith. His church is a testimony to the fruit of the trained laity. *Evangelism Explosion,* the handbook which he wrote for training laity, is now translated into many languages. The movie of his story, *Like a Mighty Army,* has been shown to multiplied thousands. Jim and I are together three or four times a year on different programs. One thing which comes through loud and clear when you are around him is that he is not the "witnessing type." He is quiet and reserved. He would rather be working on a Greek translation than talking to people. He is a walking testimony to the fact that being a witness is a matter of learning to be faithful with what God has given you. The shy and the outgoing, the introvert and the extrovert, the withdrawn and the gregarious all can be used of God.

Another thing I'm sure of is that a person can improve his skills in telling his own story. I don't mean that you can create something out of nothing. I can still remember the young ministerial student asking me, "What is it that churches go for now?" From the tone of the question, I had the feeling that he was willing at least to try to become whatever it was they wanted. He seemed a bit disappointed when I assured him that churches were not looking for certain "types" but wanted pastors who were their own best selves. That's really what is involved in learning to tell your own story. And this begins with being relaxed with your background and honest about your experiences. One of my teachers at the seminary warned us one day, "If you had a striking experience with God, write it down and reread it occasionally. Otherwise the story is apt to grow on you." He was trying to underline the absolute importance of honesty.

There are some helpful principles which you might consider in learning to share with others. (1) *Let the main focus of your testimony be on the NOW of your experience with Christ.* The word "salvation" in the New Testament is the all-inclusive word which describes all that God is doing in your life. Included in this word is the idea of conversion and all that leads to it. Included also in this word is the Christian life and all of its implications and the consummation or the end when we shall be made perfect. There is a *past* and a *present* and a *future*. It is unfortunate that when many of us think and talk about salvation we think only of the beginning or the end. We either talk about when we were converted or when we get to heaven. This is like having a Christian Home Week in the church and only discussing "how to plan a wedding" and "hints for celebrating the fiftieth wedding anniversary" with no help for all the marriages which are being lived now. The witness needs also to have a now quality.

When the apostle Paul stood before the group and told of his conversion, he was telling it to explain why he felt and acted the way he did in the "here and now." When we talk to people about our conversion, they have a right to know how things have worked out. This is really not as difficult as it may sound. It is not a question intended to embarrass you because you're not perfect. It is an opportunity to tell what Jesus Christ means to you right now.

I had the question best put to me by a stewardess on a flight from Washington to Los Angeles. The equipment had been changed to a smaller plane than had been scheduled so all the stewardesses were not needed. Those who were not working the flight "dead-headed" back to Los Angeles as passengers. One of them sat by me. She was reading a book on transactional analysis and I was working my way through *Future Shock*. We began to visit.

She was a modern girl in every way. Though she was from a solid family she had decided that marriage was passé. She and her boy friend had an apartment together, but neither of them was ready for marriage. He felt that there wasn't anything after death, but she wasn't so sure. When I told her that I was a minister she had two questions. First, she wanted to know why I had decided to be a minister. I told her as simply as I could of the experience I had as an eighteen-year-old who was crippled with arthritis and thought the end of my world had come. And then I discovered that God had a wonderful plan for my life.

She listened with interest and then hit me with the big question. "Now tell me as simply as you can, what it is that Jesus Christ does for you right now?" This is not the question that we are often asked, but it is the question which is on the minds of the people we are around. You see, they feel that if Christ can help you in the "nowness" of your life, then maybe he can help them.

I know you're curious about how I answered the girl's question. We talked for an hour but let me share with you a brief statement of the main points. I must confess that putting into words what Jesus Christ means to me to tell a person who did not have a church background was a challenge. It made me put together in one conversation many things which ordinarily would have been kept separate.

I told her: "There are several things which Jesus Christ does for me right now. First, he helps me accept the fact that I am not perfect. I make mistakes. He forgives my sins day by day as I confess them to him. Second, he helps me to accept the gifts I have and to use them in a way that gives me a sense of fulfillment. Third, he helps me to love people that I would not have loved before. Fourth, he gives mc good friends in the church who love me and care for me in all the circumstances of life. Fifth, he gives meaning to my life beyond my self. Finally, he helps me to accept the fact that I am mortal and will someday die. He gives me the hope of everlasting life through his resurrection."

Looking back on the conversation there are many things I left out. I should have mentioned the difference Christ makes in my home and other things. I have a feeling that you will not have much trouble thinking in very concrete terms about the difference Christ makes in your life day by day. This ought to be very much a part of your witness.

(2) *Try to translate your witness into words which could be understood by a nonchurchgoer.* This does not mean to abandon completely the terminology of the Bible. What I'm urging is that we be sensitive to the fact that we all tend to develop an "inside" vocabulary which is more oriented to our Christian friends than it is to those we want to win. We need to develop the capacity to listen to one another and to ourselves critically and ask, "Would a person who hadn't been to church all his life really understand that?"

Jesus came into a world where religious communication had become so specialized and technical and full of quotes that it had lost both its authority and its ability to communicate with people where they were. Then he began to describe man's lostness, not in difficult theological categories but in the pictures of the rebellion of a son against his father.

He talked of God, not in philosophical categories and definitions, but he described him as a loving, waiting father. The analogy he used to describe men's reaction to his teachings came not from a textbook on psychology but from a sower scattering his seed in the field. He used the flowers to teach of God's providence and the natural love of a parent for his child to talk of the Father's love. If our Savior was comfortable explaining God in understandable terms, then we should try to copy him.

The many modern translations and paraphrases of the Bible should encourage Christians to launch out in an honest effort to state in popular and understandable terms what God is doing in their lives. People as a rule don't use technical theological terms. It takes most of us years of maturing before we realize that some very profound religious experiences are often stated in very nontheological terms.

I recall, with some chagrin at myself, a wonderful experience my mother had when I was a young ministerial student. She had gone through a difficult period in her life and had drifted away from a closeness with God. In one particular service she came to the altar in a meaningful rededication of her life. She was quite emotional and the pastor, not thinking how difficult it might be for her to express what she was feeling, asked if she had anything to say. She said, "I know that God once saved me and that he can do it again." My mother was not trying to write a textbook on the nature of salvation. She was trying to bear testimony in the middle of an experience of God's continuing love. Of course, in my own immaturity, I was more concerned with her theology than I was happy with her new relationship. We need to look behind the words to the meaning of the experience.

(3) *Give sufficient details in your sharing that people can see you as a real person.* On the surface this may not seem important, but it can be the difference between communication and not being believable. Notice the apostle Paul's attention to precise detail in the telling of his story. He told his nationality, the town and state where he was born, where he was reared, who his teacher was, what he grew up believing, the precise details of his persecution of the Christians, the exact wording in his confrontation with Christ, the role Ananias played, and all that had happened afterward. Biography needs details if it is to be believable.

Once, when I was a teacher of evangelism, I had students stand in class to tell their fellow class members of their own experience. This can be a traumatic experience because it has not only the element of sharing but of reciting. I can still remember one young man who stood when he was called on and with one breath blurted out, "I'm so glad Christ saved me. I was twelve and I've been happy ever since." With that he sat down.

Of course the class knew the experience he was alluding to, but the witness did have a certain "ho hum" effect upon the class. In an effort to pull him out a little more, I asked if he would like to give a few more details about himself. He told me that he didn't think that he should talk about himself but about Jesus. His motive was good but his conclusions were not. By so abbreviating his experience that it could have belonged to *anyone,* he left the impression that it had happened to *no one.*

Finally, I asked if I could put some simple questions to him. I asked, "Where are you from?" He replied, "Amarillo, Texas." Right away we had him in this world. The average non-Christian thinks Christians are from some other planet. To the question about what his father did, we learned that he worked for the railroad. His answers revealed that his mother was the religious one in his family and that they had walked two miles every Sunday morning to a little Sunday School where he first was taught the Scriptures. As answer after answer was given you could almost feel the class identifying with this very real person who had sounded so unreal in his original testimony. I'm not talking about profound theological details. Where you lived, how you grew up, what your home was like, who the people were who influenced you, some of the thoughts you had, some of the details of your decision, some of the things which have happened to you since then. These are the details which make your witness easier to believe and to identify with.

It would be impossible for me to encourage you too much at the point of the potential of your own testimony. You may be a person who has never thought much about your own story. Take some time and think in specifics about what Jesus Christ means to you right now. It would be a painful and helpful discipline if you were to try writing down, just for yourself, something of your experience with God.

I once taught a class of wonderful laymen and we used one whole evening to discuss principles for sharing our testimony, then we took time to let every person write an abbreviated testimony of one page on both sides. Each person was given thirty minutes to think about his experience and then to write it down. They were organized loosely around the completing of four statements: (1) I have not always been a Christian. . . . Here they told something of their background. (2) God showed me my need by. . . . Here they told of the influences that made them think of their spiritual condition. (3) I made a personal commitment to Jesus Christ. . . . Here they told of the first steps of faith and confession. (4) The difference Christ is making in my life. . . . This was the main part and was the emphasis on the "now." Most of the people in the class, though many had been Christians for years and some were leaders in the church, said that they had never before put into words their own experience. Some who were members of the church had to admit honestly that they had never really made a commitment of their lives to Christ and became Christians as a result of being asked to write down their testimony.

Let me encourage you, in the worlds in which you live, to be sensitive to the potential of the loving word of witness to be used by the Holy Spirit to point someone to the heavenly Father. Learn to tell your story.

4
YOU'RE NOT ALONE
John 16:8-14

From earliest childhood no fear is so pervading as that of being left alone. This fear continues into adulthood in many areas of our life.

This fear struck at the heart of the early disciples as Jesus began to talk about going away. The possibility or even the wisdom of his leaving them was more than they could grasp. They needed him. Every day new insights and understandings were breaking in upon them. They were discovering that they were really just on the edge of it. There was so much more to learn.

It was at this point in his relationship with them that Jesus began to talk about the Holy Spirit. He was trying to reassure them that his physical absence would be more than compensated for by a gift he was going to send. The reassurance which he tried to communicate to them again and again was that they were not going to be left alone. This is why even after the resurrection when he was sending the believers out to disciple the whole world, he closed the commissioning service with the promise, "And, lo, I am with you alway, even unto the end of the world" (Matt. 28:20, KJV).

Those of us who live in the twentieth century have our own anxieties about being left alone. We live in a world which intimidates us. There is a kind of reckless arrogance with which secular man rushes through life. Evil seems to be more aggressive in recent years. People are preoccupied with "things," and the mere mentioning of spiritual values seems to be an interruption. There is a craze for physical pleasure which would make the early Epicureans blush. It *is* true that it is not illegal to be a follower of Christ and it is not against the law to share our faith. But those of us who have been given the responsibility of evangelizing our generation experience some of the identical needs of the early disciples. *We do not want to be alone.* We need his power and presence. And the wonderful truth is that the words of assurance to his disciples are words of comfort to us. That he is not here physically does not mean that we cannot experience the power of his presence through the Holy Spirit.

The New Testament is pervaded with teachings about the Holy Spirit. Before we deal specifically with the role of the Holy Spirit in evangelism, I would like to list very briefly some of the many emphases in the Bible on the subject. This will only introduce them and will not be an in-depth or exhaustive study. The purpose is to set in context some of the many functions of the Holy Spirit so that we will be able to relate them properly to the main task we are studying.

(1) The Scriptures teach that the Holy Spirit is given to each believer at the time of his conversion. While this is taught throughout the New Testament, nowhere is the invitation and the promise clearer than in Simon Peter's statement on the day of Pentecost, "Repent and be baptized, everyone of you, in the name of Jesus the Messiah for the forgiveness of your sins; and you will receive the gift of the Holy Spirit. For the promise is to you, and to your children, and to all who are far away, everyone whom the Lord our God may call" (Acts 2:38-39).

(2) The Scripture also teaches that the Holy Spirit is given to us in order to produce in us certain characteristics. God is interested in making us to be a certain kind of people in our attitudes, speech, and conduct. The apostle Paul clearly articulates this in the famous passage in Galatians. After listing the harvest that is reaped if we follow our natural impulses, he lists the fruits which the Holy Spirit is trying to bring into our lives: "The harvest of the Spirit is love, joy, peace, patience, kindness, goodness, fidelity, gentleness, and self-control. . . . If the Spirit is the source of our life, let the Spirit also direct our course" (Gal. 5:22-23,25).

(3) One of the best-known works of the Holy Spirit has to do with "ordaining" the church. This is recorded in Acts 2. Most Christians are familiar with it. This seems to be one of the few unrepeatable events in the life of the church. The Holy Spirit was launching the infant church into a worldwide mission with the miracle of the languages and the manifestation of great power.

(4) Throughout the book of Acts there are instances of the Holy Spirit coming to the church to give it special power. One of many examples is found in Acts 4. The particular incident takes place following the release of Peter and John with orders not to testify any more about Jesus Christ. In a prayer meeting the church was celebrating the apostles' release, praising God for his power, and asking for God's help. The record states: "When they had ended their prayer, the building where they were assembled rocked, and all were filled with the Holy Spirit and spoke the word of God with boldness" (Acts 4:31).

I am of the firm conviction that God still endues his people with power for the purpose of making his witness more powerful. Several years ago I was on the program for the Baptist Student Convention which met in central Kentucky at Elizabethtown. The Saturday evening program was to be a panel discussion by some students, special music, and a formal address by a staff member from the Division of National Student Ministries.

After the panel and the music, the speaker was introduced. He came to the podium and paused a moment to get his notes adjusted. Before he could say a word, someone in the back of the room began to sing a very familiar hymn. Of course, we were all shocked. We weren't sure it was really happening. Then before anyone had a chance to do anything one of the football players attending the convention came weeping to the front, accompanied by his campus minister, and they knelt just below the speaker and began to pray. Others began to come and kneel. Some were accepting Christ. Some were making new dedications. Others were committing themselves to vocational Christian service. For more than forty-five minutes everyone in the room felt the power and presence of God in their lives. The great spiritual upsurge still taking place on the campuses in Kentucky flows from this experience when some Christians were "endued with power." The speaker who was introduced never delivered his message, but the Holy Spirit was present.

(5) The Holy Spirit also gives gifts or talents and abilities to individuals. First Corinthians 12 deals with this wonderful truth. This classic statement reminds us that even in our great diversity we have a unity in the common source of our gifts.

(6) The New Testament also discusses the Holy Spirit in relation to "ecstatic utterances," which is a much better phrase to use than "unknown tongues." The most thorough discussion of this phenomenon is found in 1 Corinthians 14. While sincere Christians are divided over the role of "tongues" in the life of the Christian today, even a cursory reading of this chapter would remind us that this gift was

never meant to be divisive.

While all of the aspects of the work of the Holy Spirit in the world and in the life of the church and individual Christians are helpful, there is still the question: What is the role of the Holy Spirit when I am trying to communicate to others about Jesus Christ? That is a good and valid question.

Some eighteenth-century believers became so fascinated with the doctrines of the sovereignty of God and predestination that they came to the conclusion that evangelism was entirely the work of God and man ought not to be involved. Our generation has gone to the other extreme. We have become so fascinated with techniques of communication that we have almost decided that the work of evangelism is man's alone. Neither of these extremes is acceptable. God from the beginning has made his children a part of his plan. And from the beginning he has promised to be with us as we bear witness. In what ways is the Holy Spirit present when we witness? What is our part? What can we count on God to do?

1. First, the Holy Spirit is the one who convicts individuals of their sins. When our Lord was assuring the early disciples that he would not leave them alone, he spoke with some detail about just what the Holy Spirit would do. The discussion is recorded in John 16. Referring to the Holy Spirit, Jesus says: "When he comes, he will confute the world, and show where wrong and right and judgement lie. He will convict them of wrong, by their refusal to believe in me" (John 16:8-9).

There are several helpful truths in this passage. One is that the Holy Spirit convicts of sin as we share Jesus Christ. Christians do not have to be always telling men that they are sinners. We are to be sharing with them Jesus Christ.

This alone gives the Holy Spirit the tool he needs to convict men of their sins. Before men can turn in faith to the Son of God they must see themselves as they really are and turn in repentance. The truth which judges men is the sinless Son of God, and the Holy Spirit uses him to bring conviction to the hearts of individuals.

The Christian must never be judgmental in his relationship with others. He must be loving in his spirit no matter what kind of person he is dealing with or under what circumstances. We are not talking about compromise but compassion. Jesus was a perfect person. Yet the sinners felt much more comfortable in his presence than they did with some of his disciples. A classic example is the difference in the attitude of Jesus and that of his disciples toward the Samaritan woman (see John 4). He was comfortable enough with her to discuss both her husbands and his heavenly father, both water from the well and living water. The disciples had all sorts of hang-ups about her, and their judgmental attitude showed through to her. We must constantly be guarding ourselves against the "holier-than-thou" spirit which is so easy to come by and is so deadly to an effective witness. We should share Jesus Christ in love and in the power of his Spirit and leave the convicting to the Holy Spirit.

One other thing we should guard against is mistaking a casual admission of being a sinner as Holy Spirit conviction. There is a tremendous difference between a person admitting that he is a sinner and the Holy Spirit convicting him of his lostness. This is a distinction which I failed to make as a young Christian. I had not learned to distinguish the difference between things people would agree to with their minds and those they really felt in their hearts.

In talking to a person about becoming a Christian, I would usually begin by reading to them Paul's conclusion about the spiritual condition of man recorded in Romans 3:23, "For all have sinned, and come short of the glory of God" (KJV). Then after a brief discussion of the inclusiveness of the word "all," I would get from them an admission that they must be sinners since the Scripture says "all have sinned." My mistake was that I accepted this admission for conviction. However, there is really more involved than a casual and often reluctant admission.

The difference between mental assent and heartfelt conviction is very great. Let me illustrate it in the area of the marriage relationship. Suppose an individual is speaking to a couples' meeting and asks all the imperfect husbands to stand. What is he really asking? He is asking *all* the married men to stand. There is really no difference between being married and being an imperfect husband.

As these men stand in admission of their imperfection will they burst into tears of repentance and begin asking their wives to forgive them for all of their shortcomings? Probably not. They are much more likely to stand grinning at each other because they are all in the same boat. They will even find a certain humor and camaraderie in their mutual imperfection.

But if on the way home from the meeting one of the wives begins to discuss with her husband some particular aspect of his imperfection, that is a different situation altogether. Immediately the husband becomes irritated, uncomfortable, unhappy, and a bit defensive. What is the difference? In the first place he made a very inexpensive confession that he was like everyone else. But now someone who loves him is pointing a finger at his shortcomings. The emotion is entirely different.

This is the difference between admitting you are a sinner and the Holy Spirit's bringing conviction. King David proba-

bly never thought of himself as perfect, but this did not lead
to repentance and a new relationship with God. But when
the voice of Nathan the prophet became the voice of God
and he heard, "Thou art the man" (2 Sam. 12:7, KJV), it
was a different story. His body, his mind, his will, and all
his emotions were involved in this awareness. If we are faithful to present Jesus Christ in love and in the power of the
Holy Spirit, then we can rely upon God to convict individuals
of their sin.

2. Second, the Holy Spirit convinces people of the truth
of the gospel of Jesus Christ. I'm sure that the disciples had
many of the reservations which Moses had when God com-
missioned him to go speak to Pharoah. Moses wasn't too
sure Pharoah would believe him. This is why God assured
Moses with certain signs. Our Lord's assurance to us is recorded in this conversation with the disciples about what the
Holy Spirit would do. "When he comes who is the Spirit
of truth, he will guide you into all the truth; . . . He will
glorify me, for everything that he makes known to you he
will draw from what is mine" (John 16:13-14).

It is the responsibility of the faithful witness to present
to others *the person of Jesus Christ.* Our main story is not
ourselves or the church or the Bible—it is Jesus Christ. It
is good to live our lives before people. It is good to establish
meaningful relationships with others. It is good to invite our
friends to go with us to Bible study or worship. But it is
as we point them to Jesus Christ that the Holy Spirit is given
an opportunity to bear witness to the truth of the gospel.

A Christian needs to have as profound an understanding
of the gospel as is possible. While most of those involved
in the "Jesus movement" have had great interest in the Bible,
I've been with a few of the "Jesus people" who used his
name as a slogan but had no real interest in the historical

person. There is no way to divorce the name of Jesus from the historical person who came to reveal the Father's love. Consequently, every serious witness ought to seek to know more and more about the life and teachings of Jesus Christ in order to present him more fully. But we must also realize that after we present him it is the Holy Spirit who convinces the heart of the unbeliever concerning the truth of the gospel.

This is a hard fact for many educated Christians to live with. Each vocation has its own built-in temptations, and the temptation of the educated mind is to have too much confidence in human reason. Christianity is a thinking man's religion. We are to love God, not only with our hearts but with our minds. But Christianity is mainly what God has *revealed* of himself through Jesus Christ and not what man has *reasoned* of God with his mind.

I recall that while I was a pupil of the distinguished professor, Dr. John Newport, that the class was reading Emil Brunner's book, *Revelation and Reason.* Dr. Newport was quick to point out that the order of the words in the title reflected the entire thesis of the book—revelation is always above reason. With our minds we can at best establish a high degree of probability. The Holy Spirit brings *certainty.* Reason teaches the mind to say "I think." The Holy Spirit brings the heart to affirm *"I know."*

Every young Christian goes through a period when he feels the need to prop up the gospel with "proof." I suppose that living in a scientific era like this it would be unnatural to think otherwise. I well recall when this desire came to me so strongly. I was a sophomore in college and attending a state university. While I had many splendid Christian professors, I had one particular man who almost daily challenged my faith. He always smoked a pipe as he lectured. He would walk up and down in front of the class puffing away on his pipe and lecturing on psychology.

One day he was discussing radical changes in personality and scoffed at the Christian concept of conversion. He announced that he did not think the apostle Paul had really been converted but that he either had a sunstroke or was an epileptic who had a seizure and mistook it for a religious experience. He paused for effect after the statement and then he came and stood in front of me and said, "Kenneth, what do you have to say to that?" My anger at the man was only exceeded by my absolute ignorance. That's a bad combination—to be both dumb and mad! At that precise moment I determined that I was going to begin studying so that I could not only explain in detail the Christian religion but would be able to *prove* it was the true faith.

When I arrived at the seminary I majored in philosophy of religion which seeks to bring the mind to bear on every aspect of religion. I learned with delight all of the rational arguments for the existence of God and for immortality. I learned that most of the questions my professor had hit me with were not new but had been asked for centuries. I also learned that all these questions had answers. But the farther I got into the field the more I became aware of the limitations of the mind. While the mind was useful in clarifying and organizing truth into categories and applying that truth in all areas of life, I discovered that the mind did not establish truth. Ultimate truth is revealed by God through Jesus Christ who said, "I am the way; I am the truth and I am life; no one comes to the Father except by me" (John 14:6).

The faithful witness is to *present* the gospel. It is the work of the Holy Spirit to prove to the heart the truth of the gospel. Man's basic problems are not of the mind but of the heart. It is not so often a problem of the understanding as it is a problem of the will. We are not alone as we seek to share the gospel. The Holy Spirit is there to attest to its validity in the hearts of men.

3. Third, the Holy Spirit calls people to conversion. I bear witness of Jesus Christ and the Spirit convicts of sin. I share what Christ has done for the sins of men and the Holy Spirit convinces of the truth of the message. Then I invite men to commit their lives to Jesus Christ and the Holy Spirit comes and makes a response of faith possible.

I do not convert anyone. I do not save anyone. I do not talk anyone into becoming a Christian. I invite in love, and the Holy Spirit draws them to God. This idea of the Holy Spirit calling men to faith is illustrated in Peter's reference to "everyone whom the Lord our God may *call*" (Acts 2:39). Later in the same chapter Luke writes, "And day by day the Lord added to their number those whom he was saving" (Acts 2:47).

Not long after I became a pastor someone gave me my first book on how to witness. I felt so inadequate in verbalizing my faith that I was desperate for help. The author, who had a background in some phase of selling, had taken the same approach used in selling his particular product and had applied it to personal evangelism. It was full of all sorts of psychological gimmicks.

One particular bit of advice which I still remember was that one was never to ask a question which could be answered with a "no" because this would create a negative mood. The gist of this particular part of the book was that I was to ask a whole series of questions that could be answered with a "yes," building up to the final question about becoming a Christian. The inference seemed to be that the way to win people is to get them to nodding their heads on routine questions and then slip the big question in before they have time to think about it. Of course, this whole idea is an insult to a person's integrity and a gross misunderstanding of the role both of the witness and the Holy Spirit in a person's conversion.

Think for a moment about how our Lord dealt with individuals whom he was trying to point to the Father. He did not use "hidden persuaders" to trick them into the kingdom. Had he used this approach he would never have risked discussing her past with the woman at the well or suggested that there was anything lacking in the rich young ruler or confronted Nicodemus with the need for a spiritual birth. Nor did he keep lowering the standards for discipleship until he got a "buyer." He was willing, as was the case of the rich young ruler, to let some individuals go. He never once violated the will of a person, no matter how much he loved them or wanted them to follow him.

We should learn from our Master not to be afraid to be direct in our sharing and in our inviting. Most of us are far too subtle. We are too vague. We are too circuitous. There is absolutely nothing wrong with speaking directly to a person about God's love for them, and it is not unloving to ask them if they are ready to commit their lives to Jesus Christ. But, having borne our witness and given God's invitation, we must leave it to the Holy Spirit and the will of the individual to respond. I am personally convinced that there are more people ready to respond than there are Christians inviting. But we have been successful when we have shared Christ in love and in the power of the Holy Spirit. We must leave the results with God. Consequently, it is always unbecoming of a Christian to say, "I won Joe to Christ." You witnessed— *God won.*

It is an awesome responsibility which the heavenly Father has given us—to bear witness to all the world. So many times we are going to feel inadequate as we live our lives, as we relate to people, as we want to love and to communicate with them. We should remember the promise of his power. When the apostle Paul was writing to his Christian friends in Ephesus, he raised a question in essence, What is the power that was and is available to those of us who follow Christ. Then he answered with this fantastic statement: "They are measured by his strength and the might which he exerted in Christ when he raised him from the dead" (Eph. 1:19-20). It is because of this power operating in us and around us and through us that we are never alone when we share in Jesus' name. The Holy Spirit will convict of sin. He will convince people of the truth. He will call them to conversion. You are not alone.

5
LET THE BIBLE TELL
ITS STORY
Acts 8:26-40

Several years ago I spent a weekend with a group of very sharp and committed Christian students. Each of us on the program addressed the entire group, but we were also assigned to one of the cabins to lead a discussion. The first night we got into a very exciting discussion about the ministering church. The group was all turned on to the hurts of humanity and had dozens of excellent ideas about how the church could act out the gospel with a meaningful ministry to persons.

On the second night I decided that I would steer the discussion away from the corporate responsibility of the church toward an emphasis upon individual faith. I set up the following imaginary situation and then asked each one in the group to tell me how he would react. Imagine a person with whom you already have a good relationship. Suppose this person is not a Christian but has been interested enough to attend church with you occasionally and has even been appreciative when you shared something of your own personal faith with him. Once you even brought up the subject of his becoming a Christian, but he said that in spite of his interest he wasn't ready yet. But now he calls you one night and asks if he can come over. When he arrives, he has his Bible in hand.

He announces to you that he has decided that he is ready
to become a Christian and hands you the Bible saying, "Show
me in here what I need to do." Having set up this situation,
I asked each person to think for a minute and then share
with the group exactly what he would do. The responses were
very surprising.

The first person said, "I believe I would call the pastor."
A lot of people feel that lay evangelism is some layman calling
the pastor and giving him the name of someone to visit. The
second person said, "I would tell him that he really didn't
have to become a member of my particular denomination."
I assured him that the friend had not come over to discuss
denominations. This was an interesting response in the light
of the fact that the individual in the situation had taken the
initiative himself. It was interesting to me that this highly
sophisticated group of students whose whole outlook on life
had been conditioned by their relationship to Jesus Christ
did not know enough about the Bible to guide a person into
the simplest understanding of its message.

How would you have responded? Your first thought might
be that no such situation would ever present itself. But the
truth is that from the beginning God's children have been
given opportunities to use the Scriptures in pointing people
to Jesus Christ.

One of the earliest such incidents involved a young deacon
in the early church. His name was Philip and the incident,
which has some valuable lessons for modern Christians, is
recorded in Acts 8:26-40. On the surface this situation had
a lot less going for it than the one I described to the students.
Philip and the eunuch did not know each other, so there
was no friendship to draw from. The eunuch had not had
an opportunity to observe the life of Philip. There was not
any ministry which needed to be performed for the eunuch.

There was not time to develop a deep relationship. Yet in this account we see a wonderful example of using the Scriptures to point a person to God.

Note several aspects of this incident which have relevance for us. (1) The man had an interest in spiritual things. He was on his way home from Jerusalem. He was a Gentile who had turned from the many gods and the loose morals of the pagans to the one God and the more austere morality of the Jews. He probably was not a proselyte but what was called a "God-fearer." (2) He was already interested in the Scriptures. At that time the only Scripture available was the Old Testament. He had in his hand a scroll on which was printed Isaiah and he was reading aloud what we know as the Suffering Servant portion of Isaiah 53. (3) Philip began with the interest the man already had and proceeded from there. The man did not understand the full impact of what he was reading, so Philip explained that the passage was not a reference to the prophet or to the nation but to Jesus Christ who had died and been raised from the dead. (4) Once he understood the meaning of the Scripture, the eunuch believed and was willing to confess his new faith by being baptized.

Legend has it that after his baptism the eunuch went back to Ethiopia and was instrumental in sharing the gospel with the whole country. At the first World Congress on Evangelism conducted in Berlin in 1966, one of the guests of Dr. Billy Graham was the Emperor of Ethiopia, Haile Selassie. As I listened to this great Christian statesman bring greetings in Jesus' name to the Congress, I couldn't help but wonder if the very faith of the man who stood before us did not have its roots in Philip, the layman's, use of the Scripture in pointing the Ethiopian eunuch to Christ.

God has given the Christian no tool for witnessing which has more potential and power than the Bible. It is a part of our faithfulness to God that we let the Bible have its proper place in our lives and that we learn to use it to point others to him. In this chapter I want first to try to help you with a realistic way to let the Bible enrich your life. Then I want to give some detailed and specific help in how to use the Bible in witnessing.

When I was nine years old, my parents moved from the little farm on which we had been living in northeastern Oklahoma to the Quad Cities, an industrial community on the banks of the Mississippi River in northern Illinois. My grandmother moved with us and one of the first things she did was to get me and my sisters enrolled in a little Sunday School. Because most of my church attending had been in little schoolhouse churches where the different denominations rotated the preaching and everyone met in one room to study the Bible, this was the first time I had ever had a Bible teacher of my own and a class of boys my own age.

To be perfectly honest, part of my motivation related to the great picnics and parties our teacher, Mrs. Mason, gave. But this is where I was first taught the Scriptures which tell of my sin, of God's love, of the possibility of forgiveness, of the meaning of faith, and the hope of life after death. When, in a worship service a year or so later I began to feel the need to commit my life to Christ, it was in the light of the Scriptures which I had studied and learned in that class that I made my response. I'm sure that Mrs. Mason never considered herself an evangelist, but she was. The Scripture passages she taught me pointed me to Christ and prepared me to respond to his love. Her faithfulness in teaching the Bible could well be another chapter in the "acts" of the modern day apostles.

Just as an artist must understand his paints and brushes, a mechanic his tools, or a pilot the plane which he flies, the Christian needs a good grasp of the Bible if he is to use it effectively. The Bible has but one theme—what God has done to save men. The Old Testament is mainly the history of the nation God prepared—Israel. The New Testament is the record of God's final revelation of himself in Jesus Christ. Because the Bible is our authority "for teaching the truth and refuting error, or for reformation of manners and discipline in right living" (2 Tim. 3:16), it is imperative that it become *the* book in the lives of every Christian.

We are living in a crazy day when the number of false teachers is multiplying rapidly. There is an unhealthy fascination with the occult, and the gullibility of the general populace is only exceeded by the ambition of those who would confuse frightened people.

A growing sense of uncertainty about the future has driven many people, who previously read the horoscope column for "fun," to begin to take it more seriously and to wonder if maybe their life is out of their hands. The Eastern religions, with their teaching about reincarnation, have led many people to believe that this is their only hope for life after death. When to these obviously erroneous views you add the distortions of the Bible by a preoccupation with one particular emphasis, you have an excellent reason for the serious Christian to seek to understand his Bible. Only this will help him recognize and evaluate error and turn from it. Only this will help him understand the truth and live it and share it.

But how can the average person with limited time and opportunities come to have confidence in his understanding of the Bible? Fortunately, neither a great deal of time nor profound teachers are required. Any person who can read and write and who has a desire to understand the Bible will find it within his grasp.

I don't want to demean those magnificent individuals who

have spent their lives studying Hebrew and Greek and who have accumulated vast libraries of books which explain the Bible, but we should remember that most of the New Testament was written in everyday language and was intended to be read aloud to a congregation at one sitting. It was expected that the main idea of the message would be so apparent that it would not require comment. While I will discuss later in this chapter those factors which now make it necessary for us to *study* the Bible, I'm anxious that we not view it as a book that only ministers dare to read and study. People who intend to be faithful witnesses for Jesus Christ must make the Bible a tool with which they are comfortable and effective in using.

A good first step is to get in mind something of the structure of the Bible. This will allow a person to spend his time and effort to the greatest advantage. The main focus of attention should be given to the New Testament. It is true that the only Scripture the early church had was the Old Testament. This is why Philip took the text from Isaiah and pointed the eunuch to Christ. But we, unlike the first generation of Christians, have the record of the New Testament and we should give it our primary attention.

I hope I will not offend you by giving a simple summary of the various books in the New Testament. You have probably known all this for years. But when I recall how fragmented my knowledge was even as a young minister, and when I notice how confused are many of the adult Christians who have spent years in the church, I feel that it might be helpful to some.

The first four books in the New Testament are biographies of Jesus. The first three give a more or less chronological account of the life and ministry of Christ interwoven with collections of sayings and teaching. Mark is the briefest of the three and probably was written first. But the fourth biography, John, rearranges and selects material from the life and ministry of Jesus in order to interpret their meaning to us. His purpose was "that you may hold the faith that Jesus is the Christ, the Son of God, and that through this faith you may possess life by his name" (John 20:31).

Acts, penned by Luke who wrote the third gospel, is the history book of the early church. Romans is the theology book of the New Testament. The other books were written either to individuals or to congregations, usually to speak to some specific need. They are rich in their understanding and insight and have much to offer the Christian.

Revelation is the only book in the New Testament which is written in an apocalyptic style. Written at a time of severe persecution for the church, it uses a style of communicating which is most difficult to understand. Fortunately, as far as evangelism is concerned, the most important books are the easiest to understand. There are on the market a number of very inexpensive and readable books which are introductions to understanding the New Testament. A couple of dollars and a couple of hours spent getting a framework for understanding the New Testament would be a sound investment of both money and time.

The step which will bring the most help to the Christian is in actually reading the Bible. There never has been a time when the Christian had the Bible in such readable form. I can recall that as recently as my own seminary days there were men who turned aside from their main work to devote their full energies to fighting a new translation of the Bible which they felt would "ruin" Christianity. What they failed to understand was that the most critical situation facing the church is not the potential corrupting influence of an inaccurate translation but the danger of an absolute ignorance of the Bible from failing to read it in *any* translation.

Two giant strides which have accelerated the move to get the Scriptures back into easily understood language have been the publication of *Today's English Version* ("Good News for Modern Man") and the promotion of *The Living Bible.* While we must be aware that many of these are actually "paraphrases," we should also rejoice that the Scriptures have once again become readable for the masses.

The witnessing Christian should read through the entire New Testament in each of the versions he is able to get. My favorite paraphrase is *The Living Bible* and my favorite translation is *The New English Bible.* This volume of reading will not be as time consuming as you think. First, the reading is much faster in modern English where the text is divided into paragraphs instead of verses. Second, the New Testament isn't really very long. If an individual reads only three chapters each day, which in most cases would not take more than fifteen or twenty minutes, he would be able to read through four different translations each year. Of course it will take a little longer if your reading habits are like mine. I'm not a speed reader to begin with and I can't stand to pick up a book, even the Bible, without a pencil in hand. I've found that if I come to a verse which at this particular time speaks to my need, it helps me to underline it in the Bible.

The Bible will never become old to a growing Christian. Once Jesus told his disciples that there was much he needed to tell them that they were not yet able to bear. To some degree the Bible is that way. At every level of our life and our maturity, we come to the Bible with new and different needs, and we find in the marvelous book good things we'd overlooked before. Become a reader of the Bible. Through it God will strengthen your life.

The Christian witness must also become a student of the Bible. The word "student" scares lots of people. They have visions of enrolling in courses, attending lectures, taking tests, buying expensive textbooks, and all sorts of unpleasant associations. Some of the greatest students of the Bible never saw the inside of a college religion department or visited the campus of a seminary. But they became people who moved beyond the devotional reading of the Bible to the applying of their minds and hearts to seeking its meaning for today.

While the Bible has its roots in another age and another culture, and while it was originally written in a different language, and while it uses many different forms of language to communicate—it still yields its truths to all those who are willing to study it. Some study can be done privately with great profit. There are fairly inexpensive and understandable commentaries which can be purchased by the book instead of the set. An individual wanting a firm grasp of the life of Christ can decide which of the Gospels he intends to study and then purchase a study guide. Barclay's or Erdman's little commentaries on the Gospels are good. Each one has a brief introduction to the book, an outline for the whole book, then a paragraph-by-paragraph interpretation of the book. The people I know personally who do the most private study of the Bible are those who have the responsibility of teaching it week-by-week to a class. The old adage that if you want to understand the Bible try teaching it is true.

However, I'm equally convinced that the Bible needs to be studied in the context of a group of other Christians. The Bible yields its most significant truths in the context of life. An individual is less apt to stray off into subjective and erroneous views if he is willing to submit what he is thinking to his fellow Christians. This has been the genius of the small group Bible studies, of the home Bible study fellowships, and of those classes in the church which are small enough and secure enough to have open and frank discussion. I can still remember with horror a men's class I visited where the president announced, "Our teacher will now *bring* us the lesson." Then everyone looked at his own shoes while the teacher "brought it." Aside from the Christian fellowship, not much learning was going on. Become a serious student of the Bible both privately and in a class either as a pupil or teacher.

In the context of reading and studying, the Christian witness will discover it is very easy to begin using the Bible in personal evangelism. As you begin thinking of what Scriptures to use and just how to use them, there are some simple principles to keep always in the back of your mind. First, remember the very limited knowledge of the Bible that the average non-Christian has. Things which you have known for years will never have occurred to him. Even the division of the Bible into chapters and verses to aid in its study will be confusing to him.

When I was directing the program of evangelism for my denomination, we prepared some simple Bible study material for college students to be used with "Good News for Modern Man." After a sampling of the understanding of the Bible on the campuses where they were to be used, the decision was made that we would not only put the chapter and verse but the page number as well. Don't assume that a lost person knows that the New Testament tells about Christ. Be sensitive to his limited knowledge.

Second, don't be intimidated by what you do not know or understand about the Bible. The longer you live and the more you learn the more aware you will become of the inexhaustible resources of the Word of God, but this should not make you nervous about using the Scriptures to share. My good friend George Beverly Shea was once asked by a somewhat critical person if he understood all the teachings of the Bible. In his characteristically gentle manner Bev replied, "There are many things in the Bible which I do not understand, but the parts I do understand have changed my life." This can be your position also.

Third, do not underestimate the power of God's Word when it is shared with others. In some wonderful way the Holy Spirit uses it to work wonderful changes in the lives of individuals. I can remember listening to some young students, caught up in the pride of learning, who were critical of Billy Graham's habit of saying, "The Bible says." I knew that as they grew older and found themselves confronting individuals whose lives were hopelessly bogged down, they would discover that there is more power in the Word of God to deliver than in the words of man. Though we live in an increasingly secular age, my own personal experience is that there is great power in his Word.

The basis for selecting the Scriptures to be used is very simple. They should be Christ-centered. The gospel *is* Jesus Christ. The early church summed it up in one sentence: God was in Jesus Christ reconciling the world unto himself. The entire New Testament is but an elaboration of the implications of that one truth in the world and in our lives. Consequently, it is very important that the Scriptures which are shared with an individual be centered in Christ.

The promise of God is that when we share Jesus Christ, then the Holy Spirit will bear witness in the heart of the hearer. These Scriptures need to tell who Christ is, what he did, what he is doing in the world, how we are to respond to him, and what he wants to do through our lives. While it is important to have Scriptures which tell of man's sinfulness, it is God's love and the righteousness that is possible through Christ that should be first. Paul, before he wrote the famous passages on the sinfulness of man in Romans, first announced the theme of his story: "It is about his Son: on the human level he was born of David's stock, but on the level of the spirit—the Holy Spirit—he was declared Son of God by a mighty act in that he rose from the dead: it is about Jesus Christ our Lord" (Rom. 1:3-4).

During the years I have had occasion both to use and observe other Christians use many different Scripture passages in witnessing. Some used selected verses from throughout the Bible; others limited their verses to one book and often to one chapter. I have known of one or two who would use one of the simple stories in the Bible, such as the rich young ruler or Nicodemus or Zacchaeus. It is possible eventually to develop an case with choosing and using various Scripture passages, but let me share with you several suggestions which have been used in an effective and helpful way with others. In almost every case the verses involved are few enough that it would be possible for an individual to memorize them. There is great advantage to this because you can recall them, think about them, and use them with more facility.

The first Scripture passages I learned to use were while I was a senior in high school. My Uncle Doc, who pastored a small rural church, taught them to me. They were all from Romans and he referred to them as "the Roman road to salvation." They were the key verses from each of the sections of this magnificent book. The first was Romans 3:23 which told of man's lostness. "For all have sinned, and come short of the glory of God." (You can tell that I memorized them in the King James Version.) The second was Romans 6:23 which told of the penalty for sin: "For the wages of sin is death; but the gift of God is eternal life through Jesus Christ our Lord." Then I learned Romans 5:8 which told of the price God paid, "But God commendeth his love toward us, in that, while we were yet sinners, Christ died for us." The verses I learned which told men how to respond to God's love were Romans 10:9-10 which called on men to believe in their hearts and confess with their lips. Then I was taught the marvelous passage about the security we experience in God's love in Romans 8:38-39, and the passage about the nature of the Christian life in Romans 12:1-2. These nine verses contain a profound statement of the gospel which can be used by a witness in sharing Christ. The only change I have made in the use of these scriptures is that I usually start with the passage dealing with God's love before moving to those about man's sin.

Of the four Gospels more Christians use verses from John than any other. This is natural since the book is arranged to interpret Christ to unbelievers. John 1:14 tells of God's revealing himself in Christ. John 3:3 tells of man's need to have a birth from above. John 1:12 and 3:16 tell how man needs to respond. Both John 3:18 and 3:36 tell the consequences of not believing. John 10:28 tells of the security one has in Christ. John 11:25 tells of the hope of everlasting life through the resurrection of the dead. The entire book of John is rich in incidents and individual verses which can point men to Christ.

It is not so important that a Christian learn scores of different verses, for this can be confusing to an individual with limited understanding of the Bible. But it is important that a few verses be learned and that some facility be mastered in using them. Several things are important. (1) Know where they are found and be able to turn to them with ease. Know exactly what they say, and if possible, commit them to memory. (2) Know what they mean. It is essential to have a basic grasp of the plain meaning of the key ideas in a passage. In a simple verse like John 3:16 an individual ought to know what is meant by "believeth" or "everlasting life." (3) Then a person should be able to put the teachings of the Scripture into everyday terms and apply them to life. This is why the Christian should always be looking and listening for simple stories and illustrations which make it easier to explain to others the meaning of faith and commitment and being born again. All good communicators know the value of simple illustrations and use them without apology again and again. I'm always complimented when something from one of my messages can be used by one of my members to make a bit clearer some aspect of the Christian faith.

I would like to encourage those of you who still do not feel comfortable with the whole Bible to consider using one of the well-prepared little pamphlets which is designed for this purpose. They are usually a collection of key verses from the Bible which are printed and arranged to lead the person to a good understanding of God's love and plan for his life.

The two best ones I have personally used are "Peace with God" by Billy Graham and "How to Have a Full and Meaningful Life" which was developed by the evangelism staff of the Southern Baptist Convention. But there are many others which would prove equally helpful and useful. In spite of the fact that many individuals have hang-ups about the use of tracts, when individuals begin to make a serious effort at witnessing, they often feel a bit more confidence in using a series of Scripture passages printed in a tract than they do with using the entire Bible.

I would also encourage you to get as many of your lost friends as possible involved in some meaningful Bible study. This can be a Sunday morning class or a neighborhood group which meets for coffee and fellowship and Bible study. There is nothing which the Holy Spirit uses more to prepare people for salvation than fellowship with Christians and the study of God's Word. And somewhere along the way you may find an interested friend who is ready to become a Christian. If this friend turns to you with a Bible and says, "Will you show me in this book exactly what I'm to do?" will you be ready?

6
HOW TO WITNESS TO PEOPLE WHO'VE GOT TOO MUCH RELIGION

Acts 17:22-31

One of the surprises which confronts a Christian who has become serious about communicating his faith is the discovery that he must often deal with "religion" rather than irreligion. Many of the lost people in the world already have some form of religion.

In an increasingly secular America more than 90 percent of the people believe in the existence of God. In the "swingingest" dorm on a university campus, practically all the residents list a church membership. Individuals who feel that the world is neatly divided up into Christians and non-Christians are somewhat frustrated when confronted with a parade of people who either have too much religion, or the wrong kind of religion, or a warped and inadequate view of religion. How does one give an effective witness in a world burdened down with *religion?*

There is some comfort in realizing that this is not a new problem for the Christian. The apostle Paul, the first serious witness to the world, spent his entire ministry coping with this same problem. While he functioned in the first-century Mediterranean world and we bear witness in an urban culture, there are marked similarities in his situation and ours. Because Paul was a man with a well-thought-through strategy for reaching his world, there are certain principles by which he operated which are as valid now as they were then.

The best example of Paul at work in a multi-faceted religious community is his first experience in Athens. He was there alone, having left Silas and the other members of his party in Berea to nurture and organize a little group of new believers who were going to have to live in a very hostile world. While he waited for them to catch up with him, he moved around the city. The city was covered with idols. This exasperated Paul who carried in the very fiber of his being the Jewish abhorrence of any view of God but that he was one God. A man like Paul stands out in a world where it was felt that each man decided for himself what the truth was and few people held convictions strongly enough to get mad about anything which might be going on.

Paul was not idle while he waited. He went to the synagogue and argued his views both with the Jews and with the Gentile worshipers. These were men who had been repulsed by the pagan culture and had been drawn to Judaism both by their idea of one God and their high ethical standards.

Paul also got into discussions in the marketplace with casual passersby. In these discussions the Epicureans and Stoics took strong issue with him. This led to his being brought to the Court of the Areopagus, which was an open area with a high place from which he could speak to those assembled. He addressed the group. The entire account of his talk is recorded in Acts 17:22-31. This is an accurate outline of what he said, but it probably is not exhaustive. The speech, with interruptions and discussion, could have gone on for a long time. These ten brief verses give us the bare bones of his message and afford an excellent opportunity of studying his style of witnessing in an overly religious environment.

(1) First, Paul's style reminds us that we need to be more

sensitive to and knowledgable about the religions other people have. There are several reasons for this. First, people always interpret what you do and understand what you say to them in the light of their own background. When a Zen Buddhist and a Baptist start talking about God, they may be using the same word spelled the same way, but they are bringing to it two different meanings. Unless they are sensitive to the difference in background there will be the illusion of communication but no real understanding.

Second, it is much easier to love and identify with people if we know more about their background and their beliefs. If you do not know anything about the church or sect or religious group to which a person belongs, there is nothing wrong with admitting your ignorance and asking a question. Many times I have had to say to a person, "I hate to confess it, but I do not really know too much about what your group believes. I wonder if you would mind sharing with me some of the key doctrines." I have never had a person resent my asking. I have had many who were appreciative of the fact that I was willing to listen to them. I have also found that most people are not really too sure exactly what their group believes. Letting people talk to you about their beliefs will keep you from making the mistake of thinking that everyone who has an association with a group understands it and has a strong commitment to it.

Third, it is always much easier to communicate what you believe if you know something of the other person's background. To the casual observer Paul's sermon on Mars' Hill seems ordinary enough. But to the person with an intricate knowledge of the beliefs of those in the audience, the message relates almost point by point to different erroneous views they held.

On the surface it seems that Paul's audience is so different than the one we face in today's world. But things have not really changed that much. We have our Epicureans. These are those who have made a religion out of pleasure. This early Greek philosophy also felt there was no overriding purpose in the world but that things happened just by chance. They felt that when you died that was the end. They believed that the ultimate goal in life was pleasure. While they started as a serious philosophy interested in intellectual pleasure, they soon degenerated into emphasizing the most immediate, physical, and passionate pleasure. For too many people the pursuit of pleasure has become a religion.

We also have our Stoics. They believed that God was in everything and that everything was in God. They believed in fate. They saw no difference between man and God, sin and virtue, or love and hate. Much of the witness we do will be to people who never heard of these ancient Greek philosophies, but whose life is based on them. But contemporary Epicureans and Stoics are not that difficult to bear a witness to. Eventually the emptiness and the meaninglessness drive them to more significant questions than "Where is the action this week-end" and this opens them to the gospel of Jesus Christ. I baptized a young man who had come to Christ out of the Hedonist crowd. In discussing what had disillusioned him with the "swinging" crowd he replied: "It got to the place that all the girls I picked up in the singles' bars were plastic people and all the parties I was going to were plastic parties. Then one morning I looked into the mirror and there was 'old plastic me.' I knew it was time to find the real answer."

But the majority of the people we are around are neither Stoics nor Epicureans. They are Baptists, Methodists, Catholics, Latter Day Saints, Presbyterians, Nazarenes, Holiness, Buddhists, or have any one of a score of other religious affiliations. The sad fact is that behind all these labels, memberships, and background affiliations there are people who need to know God in a personal relationship, who need a faith that is vital, who need desperately meaning for their life, and who need the wholeness that comes through Jesus Christ. The unhappy truth is that a religious affiliation which has not brought a vital faith often can become a barrier.

Many times in his messages Dr. Billy Graham has discussed how a little bit of "religion" makes it difficult for a person actually to become a Christian. He uses the illustration of the method used by medical science to immunize us from dangerous diseases. A mild form of the disease is introduced into the system in order that the body may build up an immunity against the real thing. Dr. Graham's conclusion is that many people have had just enough contact with religion to immunize them against a vital faith. This is undoubtedly true and presents a challenge to those who attempt to communicate with them.

I would like to list some groupings to keep in mind which I think might be helpful in understanding those with whom we communicate. (1) Main-line Christianity is a broad but valid grouping. Of course, within this large family there are individual groups who in their zeal feel that they are the only true believers. They tend to handle their own particular identity crisis by majoring on the differences between them and the other denominations. But while there are vast differences of emphasis in the many groups, there are some things which they hold in common which makes them to be listed as Christian groups. From the Roman Catholic church on the right to the Quakers on the left, with all the rest of us in between, there is a common emphasis upon the revelation of God through Jesus Christ, the death, burial, and resurrection of Christ, the Bible as the inspired record of that revelation, and the church as God's community of faith in the world today.

The most important distinction that a witness needs to be aware of within this broad group is the difference between the evangelicals and the nonevangelicals. Though there are those who might object to this oversimplification, the difference is mainly this: evangelicals are those churches which feel that the gospel relates in a personal way to each individual and that becoming a Christian involves making a personal commitment of one's life to Jesus Christ. This represents the theological position of the church and denomination to which I belong. Yet I'm more and more aware of how easy it is to become a part of such a church without coming to a genuine faith. Many people are in these churches because their parents were. Others came in so young that it was difficult for them to have too much understanding. I've noticed that many equate believing the gospel with being a Christian. Others have learned the vocabulary and the right answers and responses without really coming to know God in a personal relationship.

The nonevangelical churches are those who believe in Christ, the Bible, and the church—but identify becoming a Christian more with the process of coming into the church and the observing of its ordinances. They usually call the ordinances "sacraments."

A very strong emphasis is placed upon the parents' responsibility to rear the child in the nurture of the church. Often there is a ceremony of dedication accompanying this commitment. As the child reaches accountability, often around twelve, he is then given special instruction in the doctrines and teachings of the Bible and formally received into the church. In theory, this is the time the child chooses for himself what his parents committed him to as a child.

The problem with this is that the vast majority of the individuals who go through the process equate the process with being a Christian. In this atmosphere some come to a vital personal faith but many do not. I have talked to scores of individuals who were surrounded by the vocabulary of Christianity all of their lives and no one ever talked to them of their need to have a relationship to Christ through a personal faith.

(2) A second group which will be increasingly encountered will be the sect. As a whole these are groups with roots within the Christian tradition who have either drastically cut out some vital aspect of the faith, have added some revelation to the faith, or have built a whole movement on the perversion of some valid teaching. Often these groups have some relationship with Jesus Christ and the Bible which gives them the illusion of being Christian, but they add some additional or different approach which is the basis of the "sect" classification.

Christian Science, with its *Book of Science and Health* in addition to the Bible, is an effort to combine philosophical idealism and Christianity. The Church of Jesus Christ of Latter Day Saints, with the Bible *and* the *Book of Mormon,* has a private and nonbiblical view of God, man, sin, and salvation. There is now emerging a reformed group of Latter Day Saints which is moving more toward a purely biblical faith. Jehovah's Witnesses are among the more aggressive sects.

There are numbers of good books which list the different sects, tell something of their origin, list some of their basic teachings, and analyze them in the light of the biblical faith. The serious Christian witness needs to be as informed as possible about these groups and needs to be aware that they really are sects and not just other denominations within the Christian family.

(3) A third group which will be felt more and more will be the many forms of the Eastern religions. There was a time when a person who had any interest in other religions had to enroll in a course in the philosophy department in "Comparative Religions." That is no longer true.

One reason is that the world has become so much more one community. The city I live in has students, businessmen with their families, and tourists from everywhere in the world. With them they bring many aspects of their culture, including their religion. Even more important has been the fact that a number of celebrities who were bored, empty, and still seeking became interested in the Eastern religions.

The youth culture has followed the interests of its idols. This has been facilitated by the gurus' discovery of America with both its affluence and its guilt, its frenzied pace and its fascination with meditation. The sight of a sixteen-year-old guru, preceded by Madison Avenue type press agents, flying into Houston, Texas, in a Lear jet, ascending a throne in the Astrodome to inaugurate a thousand years of peace would have been pure Barnum and Bailey had it not been for the fact that so many people took him seriously.

I lectured in a class at Memorial High School where a Jewish rabbi, a Catholic priest, a guru, and several others had already lectured. I'm sure they expected me to give the history of my particular denomination. But I decided, with all the discussion about non-Christian religions, that I would do a simple summary of what Christians hold in common, in contrast to the other religions of the world. I discussed the biblical teachings about the world, history, man, sin, salvation, and life after death, contrasting the Christian teaching with various other religions. The most amazing thing about the discussion was the unbelievably fuzzy thinking among many of the students who found it very difficult to believe that "everyone *didn't* believe essentially the same thing." One otherwise bright youngster exclaimed, "you mean Baptists and Buddhists hold different beliefs?" This is the world in which you will be sharing Jesus Christ.

(4) But the largest and most difficult group to deal with will be people whose religion is "cultural Christianity." These are individuals whose "Christianity" has become so much a part of the world in which they live that they have taken upon themselves many of the goals and values of the world without even realizing that they stand in direct contradiction to the biblical faith these individuals claim to profess. Almost unconsciously they have allowed religion to mean family or country or business or personal ambition. We ought not to be nervous when we make a differentiation between religion and vital faith. Jesus came into the world and called *sin* what some men called *religion.*

How shall a Christian witness in a world of "overly religious" people? What kind of style should be used in relating to them?

First, establish a point of contact which creates a climate for communicating. This may take many different forms and have several different aspects to it. It can be costly and may bring criticism from some people. Don't feel bad. When Simon Peter got back from sharing the gospel with Cornelius he had to go before a committee to defend himself. When Paul followed the leading of God to share the gospel with the Gentile world it created enough tension that a church council had to be called. Paul articulates his whole philosophy of reaching out to people, whether they were Jew or Gentile, weak or strong, by saying, "Indeed, I have become everything in turn to men of every sort, so that in one way or another I may save some" (1 Cor. 9:22). I do not know of a more radical statement of an evangelistic strategy than that.

This approach is reflected in his effort to make contact with the people of Athens in his sermon. First, he discussed how religious they were. He made their altar to the "unknown god" the launching place for his discussion of the nature of the true and living God. Later in the message, he quoted one of their poets. Many of the commentators suggest that this was Paul's only effort at using philosophy in a sermon and that he regretted it and never did it again. The overall results of the presentation do not bear out this interpretation. I'm more inclined to feel that we have a good example of making contact in such a way as to get a hearing for the gospel.

Even more critical than developing a technique for establishing contact is developing an attitude which will create a climate for sharing. Attitudes, good or bad, communicate nonverbally. Often when we are talking with a person whose background is different, we will let our insecurities and stereotypes create a negative attitude which is hurtful. Many times we do this without even being aware of it.

I recall an experience I had in an evangelism class years ago. We were discussing the importance of learning to love people as individuals rather than pigeonholing them in our minds. We did a little word-association game. I wrote a word on the chalkboard and everyone wrote on a piece of paper the "first impressions" which came to their minds. I wrote words like janitor, Catholic, waitress, Jew, or Mormon.

As we began to share what had been written down the overwhelming impression was that of being negative. With *waitress* came words like cheap, flirt, low morals, and dumb. With *Catholic* came all the memories of the Inquisitions. It was obvious that attitudes like these would create a terrible climate for sharing God's love. Then they took the same words with instructions to write down the most pleasant association they had with that word. As they shared these impressions, a whole new atmosphere was created in the room. No one had compromised any conviction he held, but a much better climate for sharing had been created.

Often the point of contact will be the common experiences and frustrations and needs which we have as human beings. People of all religious backgrounds get sick, they lose jobs, their children worry them, they are lonely, they need friends, they have good things happen to them and need someone with whom to share. People also ask questions about life and its meaning. It is often much easier to establish a point of contact at this level than any other.

Second, it is good to give a positive straightforward witness. Two temptations must be resisted. The first is to argue. Very few people are converted at debates. Paul would have gained little by doing an in-depth analysis of the inadequacies of Stoicism or Epicureanism. The second temptation to resist is being so subtle and indirect that the individual never really gets a clear picture of what the gospel is.

On Mars' Hill Paul gave a simple and straightforward summary of the gospel. He told of God as creator; of God's revelation in Christ who died and rose from the dead; and of God's calling all men everywhere to repentance and life. This is why it is of utmost importance that every Christian have a firm grasp of the basic aspects of the good news and be able to share in an understandable way. This allows the truth of the gospel to challenge man's errors instead of our doing it.

For instance, the Epicurean believed that matter was eternal, without beginning and end. To this Paul declared, "God who created the world and everything in it" (Acts 17:24). To the Stoic, who made no distinction between virtue and sin, he affirmed, "now he commands . . . all men everywhere,

to repent" (Acts 17:30). To a whole group who felt that history
was an endless circle, he announced, "He fixed the epochs
of their history" (Acts 17:26). There is more power to judge
and to draw men to God in the positive and loving presentation of the gospel than in all the arguments of men.

Finally, we must be realistic about how people may respond to our witness. Occasionally I hear someone leave the
impression that the only reason we ever fail in our witnessing
is that we either don't know how to witness, or we don't
present Christ, or there is something spiritually wrong in our
lives. While any one of those things might be true of any
of us, it is still an unrealistic way to deal with the response
we receive.

One time the disciples began to trouble Jesus about why
certain people who heard the same gospel responded so
differently. Jesus told them the parable of the sower, which
is recorded in Matthew 13. The disciples still did not understand, so Jesus explained it to them in private. He said that
there were times when the same sower using the same seed
got different responses and the difference was in the soil
and not in the seed. The point of the parable was that the
hearer has a responsibility to hear the gospel, to understand
the gospel, and to respond with his whole being. Jesus said
that many failures are on the part of the hearer rather than
the sharer.

It is interesting that the responses to Paul in Athens were
similar to those everywhere. Some rejected the whole idea
immediately. They were either unwilling to change their
minds or their lives. Others said that they would discuss it
again. These may not have been as honest as those who
rejected. It was known that many people in Athens made
a vocation of discussing with great vigor ideas they never
intended to act upon in their lives.

I recall a college student who came to me when I was very busy and asked if I would help him come to some conclusions as to what God's will for his life was. I asked him if he was prepared to do God's will once he discovered it. To this he replied: "Oh, no. I was just interested in discussing it." He would have made a great Athenian. But there were some who believed and made a commitment of their lives to Christ and began immediately to identify with the other Christians and to learn more of their new master. This will always be true. Some will say no. Others will delay. But there are always those whom God has prepared to follow him.

In the course of a year I am in contact with hundreds of people who need more than anything else to have an experience of salvation which God brings through Christ. Most of them have a religious background. Sometimes that background has laid the foundation for my helping them. At other times it serves as a barrier. But it is a fact that I must not resent and must be sensitive to those backgrounds if I'm to be used of God.

All of us occasionally delude ourselves into thinking that there is probably somewhere we could go with the gospel where we would not have to present it in the context of some inadequate religion. This is pure myth. Man is incurably religious and in his own inadequate way reaches out to God. The Christian alone is the one who comes with the story of God's reaching out to man in love and forgiveness and life.

7
TELL ALL THE LITTLE CHILDREN
Mark 10:13-17

It was a rainy Saturday afternoon in Louisville, Kentucky. Our house was located on a beautiful wooded lot several blocks from the seminary where I taught young ministers how to communicate the faith. But on this particular afternoon I was not to be lecturing to a class of forty but trying to talk with Nancy, our twelve-year-old daughter. I must confess that my love for her and my closeness to her as her father created some tensions for me. Before she was born we prayed for her. From the moment of her birth she had been surrounded with Christian influences both at home and in the church. For several months I had felt a concern about her need to make a personal commitment to Jesus Christ. Verbal communication is not always the easiest thing in the world between parents and a twelve-year-old. So, on some trips out-of-town I had begun to write long letters to Nancy about my love for her, God's love for her, and my prayers.

This particular afternoon seemed to be the time to talk. Barbara and the two smaller children were not in. I was in the living room alternating between reading and watching some chickadees on the bird feeder. Nancy came in and sat down beside me and just sat there saying nothing.

I started our visit by telling her how she had been on my

mind for some time and asked if God had been talking to her about her own commitment to him. Moisture formed in her big blue eyes and she indicated that she had been ready to take this step for some time. She asked me to help her know how to begin. So we talked together and read again the Scriptures which are so clear concerning our response to God. There in our living room Nancy took the first step of personal commitment which was to make the rest of her life different.

Barbara and I have two other children. As a pastor now I am surrounded with boys and girls who are the children of the church members. I'm convinced that all of us who seek to help children know Christ, whether we are parents, pastors, or teachers, feel a certain sense of inadequacy and a need for help. For years in most congregations the majority of the members became Christians while they were still young children. Yet in spite of this we have given very little help to those who bear the responsibility of helping children with those first important steps of faith.

Early in my ministry I had a strong reaction to some of the approaches which I saw being taken with children: approaches which I felt were manipulative and failed to consider either the nature of the child or of the Christian faith. But it is not enough merely to react. Those of us who want to be sensitive to the children and lead them to a meaningful faith in Jesus Christ must develop positive attitudes, actions, and techniques for winning the children.

One of the most telling stories in the New Testament concerning different attitudes toward children is recorded in Mark 10: 13-17. Three very distinct emotions concerning children are displayed. See if you can isolate the three individuals or groups and state how they feel about children and how they show it.

> They brought children for him to touch. The disciples rebuked them, but when Jesus saw this he was indignant, and said to them, "Let the children come to me; do not try to stop them; for the kingdom of God belongs to such as these. I tell you, whoever does not accept the kingdom of God like a child will never enter it." And he put his arms around them, laid his hands upon them, and blessed them (Mark 10:13-16).

The first group mentioned in the passage were the mothers. All they really wanted was for Jesus to touch their children. The children were not sick and in need of healing. The mothers somehow felt that some blessing might come to the children merely from Jesus' touch. It was not uncommon, when a renowned teacher came through, for parents to want him to see and touch their children. All of us have found ourselves getting our children introduced to people who were very important to us, but of whom the children were not even aware. This desire of the parents represents a beautiful gesture and tells volumes about the direction they want to go with their children.

The disturbing group in this little drama was the disciples. In all honesty, it was a difficult time for them. Christ's work was growing by leaps and bounds. With the added success there had arisen great tension which was growing almost daily. The disciples, more than anyone else, were aware of the constant drain upon the time and energy of the Master. We do not really know their motive, whether it was being preoccupied or overly protective or insensitive. We only know that they "rebuked" those who brought the children. Lest we become a little self-righteous in our censure of the disciples' attitude, we should ask ourselves the degree to which our own preoccupation with our own problems shuts the children out.

The Scriptures' account of Jesus' response is one of the tenderest pictures we have. He was indignant toward the disciples and ordered them to stop preventing the children from coming to him. He was tender with the children. He not only held them and touched them and blessed them, but he used the trusting nature of a child as an analogy by which we can best understand the nature of saving faith.

Matthew, Mark, and Luke all record this incident and in each it is followed by the story of the rich young ruler. This has led many to believe that it was Jesus' sensitiveness toward and love for the little children that had caused him to come running to Jesus and fall on his knees before him. There is really no way to know whether this is accurate or not. However, it *is* true that through the centuries mankind has been warmed by the fact that God who has revealed himself most completely in Jesus Christ is interested in our children.

While the picture of Jesus' attitude toward children is very clear, we have very little guidance in the New Testament as to how the early church dealt with children. The faith was new. Most of the followers of Christ were called to discipleship as adults. The book of Acts tried to chronicle the birth, persecution, and expansion of the church as it grew in its understanding of the gospel and in its obedience to Christ's command to preach to the whole world. The New Testament was written so soon after the resurrection that little is recorded about how the gospel was shared with those whose parents were disciples. It is most likely that the parents who were converted nurtured their children in the doctrines of the faith. The Old Testament is full of insight into the responsibility of the parent for the religious instruction of the child, and it is likely that the early adult converts from Judaism to Christ brought with them that commitment.

The idea of a faith which was transmitted down through the generations is best articulated by Paul in his letter to his young minister friend, Timothy: "I am reminded of the sincerity of your faith, a faith which was alive in Lois your grandmother and Eunice your mother before you, and which, I am confident, lives in you also" (2 Tim. 1:5).

But there is a great deal more involved here than three generations of people "belonging to the church." It should be noticed that the words Paul uses go far beyond describing a mere tradition. He describes the quality of the faith which belonged to Lois and Eunice as being "alive." And he spoke to Timothy of *your* faith with the confidence that it too would be "alive." Paul seemed to feel that in each of these three generations the faith had been alive and exceedingly personal. This is the goal of evangelism with children: not merely to pass along teachings, doctrines, and traditions but for the faith to become alive and intensely personal. It needs to become *their* faith.

And it is this goal, and the difficulty in attaining it, which creates for parent and teacher alike, a dilemma as to what is the path of wisdom. The whole idea of "hands off" is not a viable option for those who really care. The world is unwilling to assume such a position of neutrality concerning our children. It has many suggestions to make and is not the least bit reluctant to define the goals and standards and relationships in life for our children. The parent who thinks he has a free baby-sitter in the television set is kidding himself. The tube is always selling both in the commercials and in the programming. In school, at play, and in every relationship, ideas are competing for the minds and hearts of our children. There is no place for the neutral.

Equally erroneous is the idea that a parent can decide for his child or that, given certain wholesome influences, the child's response will be automatic. While the parent has enormous responsibilities and influence, there comes a time when he must back off and let the child make the big choices. This is not easy for the parent who has made so many of the child's decisions. It can be even harder on the child who has had so many of his decisions made for him. Also, to assume that the response of faith comes automatically from certain stimuli is to fail to understand freedom of the will.

But as we walk the line between taking "hands off" our children's faith and bringing too much pressure, there is a great deal which can be done. Once you have in your mind a clear goal, it is easier to begin mapping a strategy for reaching it. A parent who has made no commitment to Christ or whose commitment is not being followed too often finds it uncomfortable either to think, talk, or pray about his child's faith. Teachers who are not growing or whose own problems preoccupy them will find themselves going through the motions of working with children year after year without realizing that this aimlessness leads to failure. But once a parent or teacher has decided that his goal for the child is to help him come to a vital life-changing faith in Jesus Christ, there is much that can be done to assure the reaching of that goal.

First, it is very important to have our own minds straight about the nature of the Christian faith. This is a bit more encompassing than some realize. (1) There is the information about God's revealing of himself in the person of Jesus. This is called the gospel or "good news" and involves not only what he taught and how he related to people but certain actions which have eternal meanings, such as his death on the cross and his resurrection from the tomb. (2) There is an understanding of the response which individuals are to have toward this gospel. This involves repentance—which is a response to our sin—and faith—which is our response toward our Savior. (3) There is the idea of public confession, baptism, and membership in the church. None of these are mysteries which are hidden from us. They are truths recorded in the Bible and available to be learned. But if we are insensitive to the nature of the Christian faith we are apt to find ourselves saying to our own or someone else's children, "I think you're about old enough to join the church and be baptized."

Because of my conviction that it is of the utmost importance that we help the children with a very basic understanding of the faith, I spend as much time as possible with the boys and girls who express an interest in becoming Christians and joining the church. I've talked with them individually and in groups. I've sat around tables and sat on the floor in my office with them. From listening to the children I've come to the conclusion that we are not communicating clearly enough with our children about the basic aspects of the Christian faith.

The children are both interested and open. I have developed a little study outline which helps them to understand the different aspects of their experience. I use a homemade flip chart, get lots of participation, never fail to get some new questions, and am constantly learning. It's one of the most rewarding things which I do as a pastor. I not only teach them, I learn from them. I also establish a relationship which is personal and a friendship which is on-going. This will allow me to minister to them better as they grow in the faith.

I call my simple study "Four Steps to a Happy Life." As an introduction I tell them about the early Christians and their motto, "Jesus is Lord." We try to translate that into meaning for them for today. I also share with them some of the adventure which was involved for the disciples who lived when it was illegal to be a Christian. The children are fascinated by how they had to work out codes for revealing themselves and identifying one another. Every child I know is interested in how the fish became a symbol among Christians. After this brief introduction, I take them leisurely through the four steps. First, you become a Christian. Second, you confess your faith publicly. Third, you are baptized. Fourth, you begin growing in your faith.

Perhaps you'd be interested in why I finally made these particular divisions in talking with the children. First, in my conversations with the children I found that practically all of them felt that joining the church made them Christians. This is why I felt it was necessary to precede the discussion of joining the church with what it means to become a Christian. I use the most familiar John 3:16. Using answers found in this verse, we discuss four simple questions: How does God feel about me? What did Christ do for me? What am I to do? and, What is God's gift to me? Over and over the emphasis is made that "the first step is the big step."

The most difficult part of the discussion about confessing the faith publicly is to help them see it in the larger context of life. The children have redefined this statement to mean, "not ever being ashamed of Jesus Christ no matter where you are." In discussing baptism there are several needs. First, the idea of baptismal regeneration has to be dealt with. There is a natural tendency to attach significance which isn't there. Next, I try to get them beyond the symbol of baptism to the reality which is being acted out: the belief about the death and resurrection of Jesus Christ and our own death to self and new birth. One of the more perceptive children, when asked to define the symbol of baptism, said: "It's like a silent movie. You don't say a thing but you act out everything you believe about Jesus Christ so everyone can see."

The whole discussion of growth is an effort to help them not to look upon joining the church as the climax of their Christian life but as the beginning. Almost anyone could sit down and work out a more adequate outline for guiding children in understanding the Christian faith. If you will do it, your own understanding will be clarified. This will make it easier for you to be helpful with the children.

Second, do everything you can to create a climate of faith for the children. While it is impossible for an individual to create faith in a child, he can create a climate which will be favorable to the development of faith.

This partnership with God in preparing a child for faith was dramatized for me when our first child was only five. We had just moved to a new house in a new subdivision. There were no trees or shrubs, and we hadn't had either the time or money to put in the lawn. The place looked pretty barren, and it couldn't have been at a worse time as far as Nancy was concerned. She was just becoming aware of the beautiful world which God had created. She would go around singing a little song she had learned in Sunday School:

> Oh who can make a flower?
> I'm sure I can't, can you?
> Oh who can make a flower?
> No one but God 'tis true!

The problem was that we didn't have any flowers. So, one afternoon I took her down to Trinity Park to see all the flowers. She had a fun time. She liked best of all the King Alfred daffodils. All the way home she kept asking if we could plant some of them. Finally, I agreed and went by the store to discover that I would have to wait until fall to get the bulbs to plant.

She didn't forget, so when fall came we went to the store to get our King Alfred daffodils. I was really let down when they showed me some dried-up looking bulbs which resembled onions. The clerk, sensing my disappointment, asked if there was anything he could do. My question was simple. Telling him how beautiful they had looked in the spring in Trinity Park, and holding one of the bulbs in my hand, I asked, "How do you get them from this bulb to that flower?" He told me everything I needed to know: how deep to dig the hole, how much bone meal and superphosphate to use, and the right mixture of sand and dirt for proper drainage.

We got the bulbs, followed the instructions, and in the spring had the most beautiful King Alfred daffodils you have ever seen. The only thing about the whole process which I resented was one friend who came by when they were in full bloom and said, "I wish *I* had a green thumb." What I learned is that whether growing flowers or training a child to love God, it's not a matter of a "green thumb." It has to do with working with God to create the kind of climate for faith.

A lot of the atmosphere which we create for faith is done in an indirect way in the home. So much of the communicating which we do is nonverbal. So many elements of the Christian faith are introduced to us in the day-by-day activities and events in the family. If a child experiences and observes love in the home, he will quickly grasp the love of God. When a child sees persons given a sense of worth and acceptance in the home, it will be easier to understand the worth he has in the eyes of God. If forgiveness is acted out in small give-and-take relationships of brother-sister or parent-child relationships, then to accept the forgiveness of God will be easier. If parents are fair and exercise their God-given authority with a sense of compassion, it will be easier for the child to submit to the lordship of Christ. The home can either lay the foundation for faith or can have a crippling effect on a child's efforts to understand and relate to the heavenly Father.

A child who is early exposed to the teachings of the Scripture will find faith easier. It is so interesting to note that when the apostle Paul was writing to Timothy about what had laid the foundation for his faith he said: "Remember that from early childhood you have been familiar with the sacred writings which have power to make you wise and lead you to salvation through faith in Jesus Christ" (2 Tim. 3:15).

No better case could possibly be made for introducing children to an early and continuing study of the Bible. A child needs to hear the most attractive Bible stories, see the best Bible-based art, and listen to music which tells the stories of the Bible. He needs to be with other children his age who are learning the Scriptures. Although the understanding of a child is limited, he can still be led to have very pleasant associations with the Bible and to understand some of the key ideas about God and man and their relationship. It is impossible to overestimate the importance of Bible study in the preparation for faith.

Of course, nothing so creates an atmosphere for faith as parents who are committed Christians. For, in spite of all those times when we feel that our children are doing exactly the opposite of what we want them to do, they are more apt to copy the faith of their parents than anyone else's.

When I was still a student I pastored a small church in the seminary community. In this church was a remarkable woman who worked with the four- and five-year-old children in Sunday School. She was a woman who, having no strong Christian influences as a child, had not become a Christian until her own children were grown and married. Perhaps this is what made her feel the way she did about her work. She was very good with the children, but her overriding compassion was for their parents. She visited in the homes and got acquainted with them. She invited them to anything which might expose them to Christ. She loved their children and this communicated itself to them.

During the years I pastored that church the majority of the adults who were converted were the parents of her children. One day she expressed to me her very simple philosophy about the children she was teaching. "Pastor," she said, "these little children are so precious. They are learning so much that will someday help them come to a personal faith. But right now, more than anything else, they need Christian mothers and fathers." This is why any approach to the training of children which ignores the spiritual conditions of the parents will fail.

Third, enlist all the allies you can in the spiritual training of your children. We so often start out with the mistaken notion that we are the only influences which will be brought to bear upon our children. We soon discover many other authorities and voices trying to be heard. We also begin by thinking that we can probably handle our child's spiritual nurture by ourselves. This is a mistake.

As we have many enemies—we also need many allies. I think that the number one ally to the family is the church. Friends and relatives help. The kind of people we expose our children to socially can hurt or help.

It is sad but true that we often see individuals who are able to help other people's children and seem to do poorly with their own. This is one of the reasons we ought to help one another. So often when I have taken the time to talk to someone else's child they say, "I don't know how I can ever repay you." I tell them, "Don't worry, you'll have a chance to talk either to one of my children or to someone else's." Every day I am thankful for a network of faithful allies who join us in seeking to communicate Christ to our children.

Fourth, deliberately develop some skills at communicating with children. I've been talking to boys and girls about spiritual matters for twenty years, and I'm learning something new all the time. But you have to start somewhere. I've developed some principles which may be helpful as long as you use them for guidelines and do not hold too rigidly to them.

Conversations with children cannot be rushed. Often the best communicating is done in the less formal context. I sometimes get much insight into a child's maturity and understanding when we are talking about ordinary things like brothers and sisters and pets and school. More and more I'm aware that a child can have truly deep emotions about something without really being able to express those feelings in words.

If you will always keep the child first in your thinking, you will not be apt to get into too much trouble. Here are the guidelines: (1) Learn to ask questions the child has not memorized answers for. This is not an effort to "stump" the child or to trick him. This will keep him from falling into the trap of thinking that becoming a Christian is learning the right answers to the questions which are usually asked. This is one of the problems with a standardized approach to children. They are bright and they soon figure us out and equate answering our questions with becoming Christians. A simple little question such as, "How long have you been thinking about this?" will give them an opportunity to express what they are really feeling. You should always guard against asking questions which communicate disapproval or which question understanding. This could create an atmosphere which would make communication difficult. But a child does not mind your saying, "Let's pretend that a friend of yours at school asks you to tell him just what it means to become a Christian. Using your own words what would you tell him?"

(2) After asking a question, let the child answer. And listen to the answer. This may sound simple, but it isn't. In the first place, we have a tendency to try to protect the child by building the answer into the question. If you're not careful you'll find yourself saying, "Do you believe that. . . ." and will fill the whole question in so completely that all that will be required is a "yes" or a nod of the head. Children are so used to our answering our own questions that they often will wait expecting us to do that.

I recall while I was still a student visiting with a pastor friend. He had been invited to talk with a small boy who kept telling his mother that he wanted to talk with the pastor about joining the church. After the usual amenities, the pastor said, "Buster, your mother tells me you want to talk to me. I'm real glad. What do you want to talk about?" Buster looked first at his shoes, then at his mother, then out the window, then back to his shoes, and finally to me. He was just sure either that we would guess what he wanted to talk about or that someone would answer for him. Finally, he started talking and he and the pastor had a most meaningful conversation.

Afterwards, my pastor friend said, "I noticed you were a bit nervous in there." I assured him that I was and told him that the silence almost killed me while he waited for Buster to start talking. His reply has helped me for years to do a better job of communicating with children. "Unless," he said, "you're willing to listen to what they have to say, how will you ever really know anything about their motives or understanding?" This is true whether talking to children or adults. Sensitive listening is very much a part of communicating with children.

(3) Use the child's answers to your questions as the beginning place for sharing. Make the transition in such a way that the child's understanding is improved without his feeling "put down." Some children have profound understanding and can express it. Others are equally sincere but find it difficult to express. Some have only partial understanding and others have some erroneous ideas. Some have motives which need to be helped.

Whatever a child expresses should be accepted with appreciation for their sharing and then used as a helpful transition to a better understanding. I can still remember the cute little daughter of one of our church leaders who came into my office and announced to me that she would like to be baptized "next Sunday." After expressing delight in her interest I asked, "Tell me why all of a sudden this is what you want to do." Without any hesitation at all she replied, "So I can take the piece of cracker and juice the next time we have the Lord's Supper." She was so open and honest in it all that I felt like hugging her, in spite of the fact that her understanding and motive were inadequate. I told her that taking the Lord's Supper was one of the things a church member did but that there was a lot more to it than that. Then I asked if she would let me tell her about the other reasons. And that was the beginning of several conversations over several months which eventually led to a really meaningful commitment on her part.

(4) Move as slowly from first interest, to profession, to baptism as is necessary in order to give the child the best possible understanding of the meaning of church membership. This is not designed to perfect the child, nor should it discourage him. If the time is used wisely, I have found that both parents and child appreciate your concern. If the only motive for delaying the child is to better prepare him

TELL ALL THE LITTLE CHILDREN

for baptism, there is little danger of losing him. Actually, since the child is always dealt with in the context of his family, this gives an excellent opportunity to bring the church and family together in a commitment to the child's future. The baptizing of a child should be viewed as the beginning and not the climax. As the child matures physically and mentally every opportunity ought to be given for spiritual maturing as well.

(5) The church and the family should work together to create a climate for decision. While there are facts to be learned and doctrines to be taught, at the heart Christianity is a personal commitment to Jesus Christ. This is a matter of the will. Different children, because of different backgrounds, different understandings, and different personalities, will be ready for that commitment at different times. All the sixth graders will not be ready to trust Christ at the same time. But if the church creates a climate in which decisions can be made, as the children are ready good decisions will be made. This ought to include opportunities for first-time decisions. It ought to include opportunities for significant up-dating of religious experience in the light of their other growth.

I'm interested in so many aspects of my children's future. I want them to have a chance at schooling in order for their gifts to be developed and used. I want them to have the advantages of living in a land where there is freedom and responsibility. I want their financial future to be secure. But more than all these I want them to have the full and meaningful life that can only come through a personal relationship with Jesus Christ. I have that relationship. I cannot give it to them or make them choose it. But, working with God and the church, I can create the climate where it is most likely to take place. That's exactly what I intend to do.

8
I AM (CHRISTIAN) WOMAN
Acts 16:13-15

Bob Fowler was leading the church prayer service. Each summer several laymen and women are asked to share with the church a Scripture passage that has been especially meaningful to them—and to tell why. Bob captivated everyone's attention by announcing that he wanted to tell us about "The Four Women in My Life."

Then he told with wit, tenderness, and compassion about his grandmother, his mother, a beloved aunt, and his wife. With the telling of each he shared a significant Scripture passage which either described them or which had been meaningful to him as a result of them. As he spoke, all those in prayer meeting found God's Spirit bringing to their minds all of the wonderful Christian women whose lives and ministry had blessed their lives. His sharing reminded us all that, while many changes are taking place in the roles of women in society, women have always been a vital part of the church's witness.

The first convert to Christianity in Europe was a woman, and the first church organized by the apostle Paul in Europe met in her home. Her name was Lydia and the whole story is recorded in Acts 16:13-15. Paul and Silas had sailed from Troas, where Paul had a vision which called him to Mace-

donia. From Samothrace they had gone to Neapolis and on
to Philippi. Paul's usual technique was to seek out the synagogue and share the gospel there. Then he would use the
interest created and the converts made as the nucleus of a
new congregation. But there wasn't a synagogue in Philippi
so he varied his technique. Luke records it in the first person
plural:

> And on the Sabbath day we went outside the city gate by the
> riverside, where we thought there would be a place of prayer,
> and sat down and talked to the women who had gathered there.
> One of them named Lydia, a dealer in purple fabric from the
> city of Thyatira, who was a worshipper of God, was listening,
> and the Lord opened her heart to respond to what Paul said.
> She was baptized, and her household with her, and then she
> said to us, "If you have judged me to be a believer in the Lord,
> I beg you to come and stay in my house." And she insisted
> on our going (Acts 16:13-15).

Luke's abbreviated account is so full of interesting detail
that you can just see it happening. That last little phrase,
"She *insisted* on our going," is so descriptive of a gracious
hostess. Later, when they were released from jail, they returned to her home before journeying on toward Thessa-
lonica.

Four verses tell us a lot about her in addition to her home
town. (1) She was a God-fearer and worshiper. In the Gentile
world there were many who had turned from the emptiness
and immorality of pagan worship toward Judaism with its
worship of the true God and its higher moral standards. Lydia
was one of these. (2) She was a woman of prayer. What
the background was which established the riverside as a place
of prayer I do not know, but it was a designated place and
she was there. (3) She was a successful businesswoman. She
sold expensive purple, made from a shellfish, with which

fine wool fabrics were dyed. (4) She was a woman who was
respected. After she committed her own life to Christ her
entire household followed suit. (5) She was a gracious hostess.
Her awareness of the ordinary need of the apostle's party
and her insistence that they come to her home tells volumes.
(6) She was a woman of courage. Entertaining the visiting
preacher was not so bad, but welcoming him and his party
back into the home after the incident in jail was something
else. That she allowed her home to become the center for
Christian activity in a town which was so Roman that it did
not even have a synagogue is a testimony to her faith.

From the very beginning until now the work of Christ and
the church has been enriched by the witness of Christian
women. One of the first instances of a woman giving a verbal
witness for Christ is recorded in the Gospel of John.

Jesus and the disciples were traveling from Judaea to Galilee through Samaria and stopped outside the town of Sychar.
The story is probably familiar to you. While the disciples
were in town, a woman came to get water. Jesus engaged
her in a conversation and she came to believe in him as
the Messiah. To this simple and sinful woman Jesus revealed
some of the most profound insights about the heavenly Father
and spiritual worship that is recorded in the Bible.

It is interesting, and just a little discouraging, to notice
the sharp contrast between the attitude of the Master and
that of the disciples. They definitely disapproved, and though
they did not say anything to Jesus, John records what they
thought. Part of their problem, though not all, was that *she
was a woman.* Judaism had a much higher view of woman
than the surrounding nations and cultures, but she was still
considered quite the inferior. Though the rabbis married and
had families, it was really considered beneath these noted
"teachers" even to be seen talking to a woman in public.

Many leaders still have the same problem which the disciples had.

Whether the woman sensed the spirit of the disciples is not known. When she returned to her village, she became an unembarrassed evangelist as she proclaimed to the people, "Come see a man who has told me everything I ever did. Could this be the Messiah?" (John 4:29). They followed her out of town to see and hear Jesus, and "many Samaritans of that town came to believe in him because of the woman's testimony" (John 4:39). The net result was that Jesus and the disciples spent two entire days with them, all because of the witness of a Christian woman.

God still uses the witness of Christian women, and there are many whose experience with Christ is fully as dramatic and influential as the woman of Samaria. Eleanor Whitney is such a woman. The first time I heard her, my wife Barbara and I were attending a banquet in New York City which was sponsored by the New York Bible Society, the parent organization of the American Bible Society. Jerome Hines, the opera star, gave a witness and sang. The speaker was Eleanor Whitney. The contrast between the simple first-century village of Sychar and sophisticated twentieth-century New York City is great, but the story she told was the same and it had lost none of its impact. Mrs. Whitney told of the experience of conversion to Jesus Christ which had taken place in her life during the first Billy Graham Crusade in New York City and the wonderful differences it had made. She urged everyone there to consider whether they ought to turn to this same Christ.

Several years later, when Billy Graham was in a crusade in the Madison Square Garden, I was in the city speaking to a group of ministers in a school of evangelism. I had dinner at the hotel across from the Garden with Maxey and Sarah

Jarman, and I noticed Eleanor Whitney come in with a large party. I later learned that each night during the crusade she had a different group of friends to dinner at the hotel. Then she took them to hear Billy Graham in hopes that God would use his message to point her friends to Jesus. The setting was different but the style was the same.

When a woman shares with others what she has come to experience because of Jesus Christ, it releases a power for righteousness in the world which can change the lives of individuals. The thing she must always be aware of is that she does not have to have the notoriety of the woman of Samaria or the forceful personality of an Eleanor Whitney to share her faith. Often a word shared with an interested friend over coffee or a "sit-on-the-side-of-the-bed" type chat with a daughter is a better platform than the town square or a banquet. I became a Christian as a small boy because of the quiet and faithful witness of Mrs. Mason, who loved and ministered to and taught me as a part of her Sunday School class.

Many women bear witness by the special quality of sensitiveness which they bring to life's needs. Such a woman was Dorcas about whom Luke records one short but telling incident. She lived in Joppa and was one of the Lord's disciples.

The account was probably recorded in Acts because after she died Simon Peter came and prayed over her and God brought her back to life. But she has been remembered not so much because her life was extended, but because of the quality of the life she lived. For Luke tells us that she "filled her days with acts of kindness and charity" (Acts 9:36). When Peter arrived in the room where her body had been laid out, the room was full of women who held in their hands the clothing which Dorcas had made while she was living. I'm convinced that it was more than shirts and coats which could be left behind which distinguished her. The things which she did flowed from a heart that had been touched by God's love. Her sewing was an extension of that love which reached into the lives of others.

There is a touch which a woman brings to a situation that would leave life impoverished if it were gone. I've tried to isolate and analyze what that special awareness is. I'm sure it is many things, but one or two stand out. The woman's touch is very *person centered.* She is not always moved by statistics and charts and graphs dealing with poverty. But when need is personified she grasps that and responds almost automatically. While men are more issue oriented, most women are person centered. Also, most women are aware of what might be thought of as "small details" in the needs of others. Often men do not understand the need for a gift to be wrapped or the individualizing of some very ordinary present like a broom or making an occasion out of an event like eating out. This awareness in women starts early.

I recall that in my student church I was the principal for our Vacation Bible School. The lady who was in charge of refreshments for the small children wanted to do something special, so she went to the store each day just before the refreshment break and bought Popsicles. As a part of making the children aware of the need to be thankful, they always had a prayer of thanks before they ate. I was in the group, and they asked a little girl who had not missed a single day to say the prayer. I can still remember that clear and excited voice as it said, "Lord, we thank you for the many Popsicles," and then after a brief pause she added, "and especially that we've had a different color each day." Only a little girl would have included that.

One of the many things which impressed me as I read *The Hiding Place* was the perspective and insight which women can bring to an interpretation of brutality and suffering and dying. It is the biography of Corrie Ten Boom and her family as they suffered because of their ministry to the Jews who were being persecuted. It looks through the eyes of a Christian woman at the horrors of prejudice, the pressures of war, the suffering of persons, and the real values and meaning in life.

The sensitiveness need not be limited to physical needs such as food or clothing. Often a woman is able to make just as permanent and significant a contribution by being sensitive in other areas.

I'm so thankful for the awareness of women in the church when there is illness and death. I sat by the hospital bed of a woman whose doctor had just told her of the recurrence of a malignancy after many years. As we talked about how she was going to handle this new and severe crisis she said to me, "Kenneth, there are some women who are my dear friends. When I first faced this years ago they were aware of all I was going through and they stayed with me and helped me. They're still my friends and I feel their support so very much. Don't worry about me. There is nothing I have to face for which God has not provided the resources." I think the confidence I was looking at in this woman's life was just as real and much more warming than a shirt or a coat. It had been woven by sensitive women out of the threads of love and concern and Christian compassion. We're living in a world that needs more than ever a woman's sensitiveness and awareness.

The Christian woman plays a most significant role in giving direction to the religious life of children. I've reached back into the memory banks of my mind, and I cannot remember a single instance in the twenty-five years of my being a minister where a Christian man, whose wife was not interested in religion, was able to lead the children to love God and to commit their lives to Christ. In contrast I can think of a score of families where a devout woman married to an indifferent man was able to be the difference in the life of the children. I must confess that these mothers who have "sole religious support" thrust upon them have some rough times when their boys hit the teen years. This observation is not made to condemn the men so much as to remind women of the incredible influence you have upon your children. You are the number one force in their life.

The Scriptures are filled with examples of the difference the religious commitment and concern of the mother had on the children. Read again the story of Samuel's mother, Hannah (1 Sam. 1:9-28). The character and commitment of the prophet was molded by the prayers and love and faith of his mother. It is true that she "lent" her son to the Lord for his whole life, but he carried the fruits of her labor in that life. Paul's letter to Timothy, his son in the ministry, indicated that the direction and quality of his faith had been set by his grandmother and mother (2 Tim. 1:5). I shudder to think what would happen, or perhaps I ought to say what *will* happen, if Christian mothers do not point the next generation in the right direction.

The influence of the Christian woman is not limited to her own children. Much of the solid religious education which has been done with children in the church has been led by dedicated women. It is good that there is a growing involvement of men and of couples working together in the children's departments in church, but this is still the exception rather than the rule. I'm of the opinion that when we finally are able to evaluate all that has been done in the church that some of the real heroines will be women who in a quiet and selfless way gave a witness for Jesus Christ by pointing boys and girls toward him.

The home of a Christian woman represents both a means of ministry and a base for ministry. Lydia's home was not merely the place where the church of Philippi had its worship services. It was the place where the food was cooked for the preacher and a bed was provided for him and his friends. In that special home in Bethany which so warmly welcomed Jesus were two wonderful Christian women. Mary and Martha ministered to the needs of Jesus even as he ministered to their spiritual needs. I could fill a book with a list of the homes and the individuals in those homes who have ministered to me.

Many of the homes in the Bible and homes today are not complete homes in the sense that they have a husband and wife and children. I've watched death and divorce both leave a home without a partner. This does not necessarily mean it is without spiritual strength. The home in Bethany had two single sisters and a brother. Whether "home" is a single adult living alone or sharing an apartment, it can be a Christian home. A parent without a partner, whether in a high-rise apartment or the old family home, can still have a home where love is and Christ is known.

The Christian woman has great potential as a Bible teacher. In every church where I've been long enough to get acquainted with the people, I've discovered there are women who have given themselves to a study of the word of God and to teaching. Some of them, though they usually lack formal training in the field of religion, gain through disciplined study and much experience both solid Bible knowledge and excellent teaching ability. Because they usually specialize in teaching one particular age-group they become the best kind of Bible teacher, the one who interprets the Word of God in the context of life.

Unlike the scholar who sits in a study surrounded by books, these teachers are constantly with women who are having babies, or moving, or trying to rear their children. Consequently, they are never studying the Bible in the abstract or merely looking for ideas which are interesting to discuss. They study the Bible in the concrete, looking for help in daily living. All over the land there are women whose life has been blessed by the ministry of a Bible study class and often these classes are but the lengthened shadow of a Christian woman who has developed her gift of teaching.

An increasing number of women are bearing witness to Jesus Christ in the context of a career. For some this is because of economic necessity and for others it represents a need more connected with a stewardship of gifts than the need for income. Many of society's most needed skills are exercised mainly by women. What would happen to the school systems and the hospitals and many other of the most needed institutions in our communities if there were no women who saw their calling as a career. I think it is important that we not make women in "outside the home" careers feel guilty, and women who make careers of homemaking should not be made to feel like traitors to the feminist cause. Neither of these will be easy.

For years there has been a steady stream of novels, television programs, movies, articles, and interviews which have left the impression that nothing is a greater waste of womanhood than the devoting of her time and talents to being wife, mother, and homemaker. She is pictured as frustrated, unfulfilled, unread, provincial, victimized, and dull. She is represented as having been shoved out of the house by modern conveniences with little to do but become a lady alcoholic, have an affair, or invent some "busy work" to do while her lucky husband is out doing "real work."

This is an unfortunate caricature. It has probably come in reaction to an idealizing of homemaking which has not dealt realistically with many of the frustrations. So many of the jobs she has just "won't stay done." There is an enormous energy drain in the process of living with children through what seems like an endless series of "stages." There are times she feels both *used* and *used up*. There is nothing unchristian about either feeling or expressing this frustration.

What the Christian woman brings to homemaking is a larger perspective. Barbara and I have discussed this. She deals very realistically with some of the many activities which in themselves are not terribly rewarding. But she feels that these are things which need to be done as a part of caring for the people she loves. If her measure of herself were just how well she did the laundry or how clean she kept the house or how promptly she served the meals, she would have a totally different evaluation.

I've observed the difference the Christian woman brings to her career of homemaking. There is a moral and spiritual dimension to her role. She has an objective basis for establishing priorities as she makes the day-by-day decisions which affect everyone's lives. Your home will be richer if you can say, "I am Christian homemaker."

At the same time, being full-time homemaker is being caricatured, the role of the career-woman is being idealized. She is pictured as fulfilled, dressing better, meeting more interesting people, being more creative, and more sophisticated. This too can be a myth. Many a woman works long hours for less pay than she would make if she were a man and stays broke buying clothes and paying for child care. She does the same thing over and over until she wants to climb the wall. So much time is spent simply taking care of routine shopping and chores when she is at home that she has neither time nor energy to read books. Often she finds herself working with self-centered people who use her abilities without having any real interest in her as a person.

I've known many women, both single and married, whose careers have been fulfilling and enriching. These persons have made a wonderful contribution to society. And I've noticed an interesting similarity between them and the housewives. They also have to put the things which they are doing into a larger context. They also live with the real difference which Christ can make in a career. The Christian woman in an organization can be a witness by the commitment she gives to her job and by how well she does it. She can be a witness by how she gets along with the others in the office or corporation or store. She can be a witness by the moral values she has in her life and relationships. It may be true that there is no such thing as Christian math, medicine, typing, accounting, or sewing. But it is true that there are Christian math teachers, secretaries, accountants, and seamstresses. And that can make a vast difference.

But whether a woman sees herself primarily as homemaker or a career woman or as combining both, she needs always to be aware of the importance of bringing Christ into all areas of her life. I observe constantly some fine women who are letting Christ be seen in and through them as they function in homes, in careers, and in the life of the church. And the combination of jobs and interests stagger the imagination. The fact that they are bringing Christ into all the areas of their lives gives them a wholeness, in a world which tends to fragment people. It gives them values and a basis for setting priorities in a world of relativity which is destroying many. It gives them a sense of self-esteem which makes it possible for them to deal with people in a loving and wholesome way. It gives them the resources for dealing with all of the littleness, disappointments, and frustrations of their work. And a woman who takes Jesus Christ into her world will constantly be coming into contact with men and women who have no such "extra" in their lives. If a woman intends to work outside the home, she will be happier if she looks at her job not only as income and fulfillment but as being a mission to persons.

I sat one evening at a banquet where I was to be the speaker. It was the annual "couples night" for a Christian woman's organization. I sat with the president and her "program chairman" (that was *her* title) and their respective husbands.

We were having the usual sort of conversation until I asked my question. It just happened that we had one of the rather colorful and vocal leaders of the woman's lib movement in town and she was getting lots of coverage in the media. I had my own private opinions about the whole affair but hadn't had the time or opportunity to discuss it with anyone. So I asked these two delightful women, "How do you think woman's liberation is going to affect you two Christian women?" It seemed like such an innocent little question, at least to me.

Both of them immediately disassociated themselves from the movement, expressed their personal displeasure with the goals, methods, and life-style of most of the woman's lib leaders, and insisted that they were not going to be affected by it. While I agree with the values expressed by these two women, I cannot believe that they will not be affected.

The reason I feel this way is because of what I've observed about the nature of movements. They tend to move the center. Let me illustrate it with the civil rights movement. Most of my friends who are a part of a racial minority neither identified with many of the leaders nor approved of their methods. But all my friends were changed. The Negro maid who goes to church in her community and rides a bus to work in another community may think that because she never participated in a sit-in and didn't even like Stokely Carmichael, that the civil rights movement didn't affect her. But the truth is, she views herself and her children and her country differently. The center has been moved. The same is true in the peace movement and ecology. I'm convinced that the same will be true of the woman's liberation movement, and it won't have a thing to do with how we as individuals happen to think about its goals or leaders or methods. The center is going to move.

I think this movement gives the Christian woman an unparalleled opportunity to bear witness for Jesus Christ. The Christian woman alone has the possibility of true liberation: liberation in the acceptance and love of Jesus Christ, liberation in the discovery and development of her gifts, liberation in the celebration of the uniqueness of the gifts of others, liberation in the awareness of the need we have for each other, and liberation in sharing a gospel of unity. This is a goal or an ideal.

There are many Christian women who have a long way to go to experience the fulfillment which God wills for them. But I'm convinced that apart from Christ all of the freedoms will be new forms of slavery. Barbara, my lovely wife, and I sat in our den watching the Emmy Award show being televised from Nashville, Tennessee. It was the night that Helen Reddy got an "Emmy" for her recording of "I Am Woman." The orchestra played her song as she came onto the stage to receive her award. I liked the song. It's strong and it moves. I also identify with the affirmation of worth and strength in it. But the song and the movement both have one word missing, it is the word "Christian." The real woman's liberation movement starts out, "I Am *Christian* Woman." This is a freedom to be shared with everyone.

9
THE WITNESSING LIFE
2 Corinthians 3:2-3

The old adage that "I'd rather see a sermon than hear one" has a great deal more relevance to evangelism than most of us are comfortable with. No truth more permeates the New Testament than that being a Christian involves both a personal experience with Jesus Christ and a life-style which seeks to follow his will. Our Lord was laying the foundation for this idea when he said in the Sermon on the Mount: "You . . . must shed light among your fellows, so that, when they see the good you do, they may give praise to your Father in heaven" (Matt. 5:16). Christ obviously wants there to be a consistency between the gospel which we share with others and the life we live before them.

When the apostle Paul was writing to the church in Corinth and answering the charge made by some that he did not have the proper credentials, he insisted that the proof of his ministry was not to be found in his "certificate of ordination" but in the lives of his converts. He said: "Do we, like some people, need letters of introduction to you? . . . No, you are all the letter we need. . . . any man can see it for what it is and read it for himself. And as for you, it is plain that you are a letter that has come from Christ" (2 Cor. 3:2-3).

Long before I had found this particular passage in the

Bible, the little country church I attended sang a song by
B. B. McKinney which spelled out the same truth in unmis-
takable terms.

> Your life's a book before their eyes,
> They're reading it thro' and thro';
> Say, does it point them to the skies,
> Do others see Jesus in you?

Everyone who desires to be a witness for Jesus Christ must
give some serious thought to the witness his life gives.

I have not been back in the pastorate very long. And it
was a rather radical change, after eleven years of teaching
evangelism and four years directing evangelism for my denomination, to find myself as the pastor of one congregation.
It has been a most encouraging experience.

One thing that I have especially been made aware of is
the close relationship between the lives we live and the effectiveness of the witness we give. During this time I have had
in-depth conversations with scores of adults who have become
Christians. In the process of helping them both to understand
and to articulate their newfound faith, I have asked them
to tell me some of the influences the Holy Spirit used to
lead them to faith. Almost without exception some individual's life has been pointed out.

Typical of these was an engineer with a worldwide con-
struction firm, a native of Taiwan, who had confessed his
faith in Jesus Christ. When I learned that he had heard the
gospel first more than twenty years before, I asked what had
helped him to believe now. Referring to one of the men
in our church he said: "For three years I have watched him
very closely. His love for people and the great happiness
I see in his life made me know this gospel is true." It is
rather frightening to realize that there are people to whom

our *life* is the witness.

There are several principles which have been passed on to me by different individuals which have helped me keep my balance as I've dealt with this idea. *First, how we live serves as a foundation for our verbal witness and not as a substitute.* I can still remember the conference on witnessing at a student convention where a cute little coed, with hands on hips, announced to me in front of the entire group, "You can talk about Jesus all you want to, but I'll just *live* my religion." She seemed to be suffering from the mistaken notion that we have that choice.

In the first place, talking is a part of living. We live in a world of verbal communication. One of the most frustrating periods of my life came when, because of some problem with my vocal chords, the doctor made me go for three full weeks without talking. He didn't even want me to whisper. All my communication had to be either sign language, which I discovered very few people understood, or writing. The craziest part of the whole experience was my discovery that when you quit talking, people come to the conclusion that you can't hear either and start writing you notes. Talking *is* a part of living.

But even more important, our lives give meaning to our words. When you hear people say that words no longer have any meaning, what are they really saying? They are admitting that certain words have been cut loose from an authenticating reality. Several years ago I found myself on the platform with a man who was trying desperately to make a case for a "voiceless Christianity." Over and over he kept saying that words had no meaning. In the "friendly debate" which followed our two presentations I suggested to him that words connected with reality were still powerful. Then I wrote the words, "Take me to Cuba," on a slip of paper and suggested that, if when he boarded the plane to go home from the meeting he would give these four words to the stewardess, it would change his whole life. Everyone got the point.

When the good news of Jesus Christ becomes flesh and bones in the context of life, then the words of the gospel become alive and interesting and powerful. When we are around a person who is so alive that he radiates it, it is not hard to listen to him. When we have seen self-giving love acted out in the ordinary relationships of life, then "God loves me" becomes believable. The validity and authenticity which God wants our words to have is undergirded by the life which we live. But this life is the foundation for our witness and not the substitute.

Second, the starting place for each of us is our own personal life. If our lives are to be mere channels through which the love of God flows, then it is of tremendous importance what kind of persons we are. This has both a negative and a positive side. Negatively, we need to ask God to help remove from our lives anything which would be harmful or misleading to others. I'm very aware that each of us is an imperfect human being. In spite of the fact that we are children of God by faith in Christ there remain in each of us areas of imperfection. And if God never used anyone but perfect people to do his work, he wouldn't get much work done.

I'm thankful that God can use frail children to do his work. But I'm also aware of the fact that all of us realize there are things in our lives which are a hindrance to our witness. It may be attitudes. It may be ways of thinking or talking. It may be habits which have too much control over us. As we share with others this wonderful love of God our lives need to be clean.

But the positive side is equally important. A life emptied of all that is questionable is still an empty life. Interpreting the Christian life in terms of "giving up" is at best half-Christianity. This is the very thing which nurtures the idea that Christianity is essentially a religion of "do's" and "don'ts." Our life needs to be filled with the fruits of the spirit: love, joy, peace, patience, long suffering, and self-control (see Gal. 5:22-23).

A realistic awareness of the progressiveness of the Christian life is of great help. When I'm dealing with a child who has become a Christian, one of the greatest areas of concern is that as he grows and develops physically, intellectually, and emotionally, his spiritual growth will match the other areas of his maturing. The same is true with each of us. As we live our lives we are aware of growing responsibilities, whether as employees, students, or parents. This is also true spiritually. In the spiritual growth process we need all the help we can get. This is why some regular study of the Bible is important. This is why a witnessing Christian needs the resources of a deep prayer life. This is why an open commitment to a church fellowship is mandatory. All these aid us in measuirng how we are doing and also assist us in being consistent in our living.

Third, the witnessing life begins with the family of God, the church. One of the first steps of an individual who has responded to the love of God is to become a part of the family of God. It is in the church that our first efforts at living the Christian life are given expression. Even a cursory reading of the first chapters of Acts reveals a style of life and a quality of community in the early church which was absolutely unique. I'm convinced of two things. First, one of the greatest needs of modern man is to find a place where he is accepted as he is and is loved. Second, I'm equally convinced that the only organization in the community which has the potential for becoming just that is the church.

A friend of mine has written a piece about the cocktail lounge calling it the "Artificial Church." He says that the whole "happy hour" mentality exists because of man's need to be relaxed and accepted and at least to feel like he is a part of a big happy family. Of course there is nothing quite as forced and artificial as the gaiety of a group of strangers sipping drinks in a dark room and getting hoarse trying to carry on conversation over music that's too loud. But the need which drives them there is as real as life. It is too bad that many of them have never been a part of a real community of love.

I know that Christians are not supposed to limit their love to one another, but this *is* where they are to start. And nothing makes it easier to take love out into a world starved for it than observing and experiencing it in the family.

I'm so fortunate to be in a church where the people have learned to live out the Christian life in relationship to one another. One of the most obvious ways is when tragedy strikes. I cannot think of a single time when there has been an accident, a serious illness, or a death in a family but that when I arrived, there were already Christian friends ministering to the needs they found.

A typical incident involves a teenager who was wounded in a hunting accident. It took place miles from the city so that none of us heard of it until just before the evening service Sunday night. I announced to the church what had happened and we stopped and had special prayer for the young man and his family. As soon as I could get away after the service, I rushed to the hospital only to discover that several families of members had already been by. They had not just come to express concern, but knowing the need of the parents to stay at the hospital during surgery, had made arrangements for care and transportation of the other children for the next day's school. This is the witnessing life. This is observable Christianity.

The other area in which it is important for us to learn to act out the gospel is when difficulties come to our fellow Christians. While the average church member finds it normal to respond in love to illness and death, sometimes he is at a loss in knowing how he should react to other kinds of problems. What should be done if a fellow member loses his job? What should be the reaction if two active members find their marriage failing, and then separate? What should be the reaction if the pastor's son is arrested or a deacon's daughter runs away from home? There are many times when our human wisdom fails us but love should not. We must learn to be loving, caring, accepting, and helping to Christians within the family of God.

Each Sunday I stand and announce to those in our sanctuary and to the several thousand in the television audience that no matter what they have done in their lives, God still loves them and wants to bring them forgiveness and hope. I also invite those who are willing to accept God's love to come and be a part of the church. What I say to them about God's love is made more believable because they see in the church the kind of loving, caring, accepting fellowship that God has created. The statement: "They met constantly to hear the apostles teach, and to share the common life, to break bread, and to pray. . . . They . . . shared their meals with unaffected joy, as they praised God" (Acts 2:42,46), need not be reserved for the first-century church. It can be an accurate description of a church today whose life is a witness to the gospel.

Fourth, the witnessing life needs to be person-centered rather than issue-oriented. If we're not very careful we will find ourselves more interested in the theology of suffering than in the sufferer. This was the case with the disciples as they noticed a man who had been blind from birth. Rather than calling attention to the unfortunate condition of the man and considering what might be done to help, the disciples raised the question of who was responsible for his blindness, the man or his parents. It was the person-centered ministry of Jesus which refused to get bogged down in a theological controversy when there was an individual who could be given sight. We should learn a lesson from our Master.

When I was teaching, I had a student who had the most sensitive radar to persons with needs of anyone I've ever known. When he left school he went to a small community in central Kentucky and began pastoring a mission in a deprived section of town. Everywhere he turned he found need—children who were sent to school without breakfast, elderly people with no one even to check on them, grown men who could not sign their names, and teenagers with no place to play.

He began to lead his small mission in meeting every need possible, and when their resources were inadequate, he hunted for outside help. One day he was in town, having brought an elderly man to get glasses fitted, and he came by my office. He had discovered the handbook of various government programs that had funds available to meet some of the needs in his community, and as the only person in the neighborhood who knew enough to fill out the endless applications, he was busy at work on them and as excited as a child with a new toy.

As we discussed some of the individuals he was trying to help, I asked him if the sheer number of people who had problems and needed help didn't sometimes depress him. He seemed almost surprised at my question and replied, "I'm so busy trying to help the people around me who need help that I don't think too much about all the others. But I have the feeling that when I reach out to the persons in front of me and embrace their need, I have within my arms the whole world."

It is true that Christians, from time to time, have opportunities to deal with the broad issues which affect individuals. This they should do. I recall more than twenty years ago hearing the great Christian educator, J. M. Price, give a talk on the importance of Christian concern in preventing injustices and abuses.

The clincher for this impressive talk was a poem about a community which was located at the bottom of a cliff where people kept falling off and injuring themselves. The community was very compassionate so they raised a sum of money and then argued over whether to buy an ambulance and park it at the bottom of the hill or to build a fence around the top of the cliff. Unfortunately, the Christian community seems to be divided along the same lines. That is sad because this is not the simplistic choice we have. Our interest in the so-called larger issues of society must never replace our sensitiveness to and interest in individuals who have needs.

Fifth, the ministry to persons needs to be in connection with the ordinary needs of life. In the Gospel of Matthew Jesus tells a haunting parable about the kind of help we should be to people. (See Matt. 25:31-46.) The setting is the judgment day when the good and bad are being rewarded and punished. The basis of the reward or punishment has to do with the way they either ministered to or failed to minister to the Son of Man. Neither group was aware either of their ministry or neglect so Jesus closes the story with the unforgettable verse: "I tell you this: anything you did not do for one of these, however humble, you did not do for me" (Matt. 25:45). But the interesting thing in this striking parable is that the ministries performed were not dramatic, newsworthy deeds. They were ordinary needs of individuals—food, drink, clothes, a place to stay, and help when in trouble. Many of us as Christians sit waiting for the big opportunity to show our religion and let the endless small opportunities pass us by. Soup taken to a sick neighbor, a phone call to a person having difficulty, a conference with the district attorney about a boy worth saving, a reference filled out for a person seeking employment, and a million other opportunities come to us all day by day. This is the stuff of which the witnessing life is made.

Often we fail to realize the small ways in which the love of God is being communicated in a nonverbal way. I had to conduct my prebaptism interview with an elderly lady with the aid of an interpreter. She was a citizen of Mexico and knew very little English, and I knew even less Spanish. She was a woman of culture and refinement. She had traveled widely and had been exposed to many religions and different philosophies of life.

When I asked through the interpreter what caused her to believe, this is the story she told. "I came to this city as a stranger and I was very lonely. One of the ladies in your church came to visit me. At Christmas she brought me a book as a gift, and she even wrapped it in pretty paper. But the best thing was that she had me in her home for a meal. When I saw the very genuine love she had for me, I knew that the story in the book about God's love was true." As I listened to her simple and powerful story, I could almost hear the Master saying of my church member, "Inasmuch as ye have done it unto one of the least of these . . . ye have done it unto me" (Matt. 25:40, KJV).

Finally, the witnessing life needs to relate primarily to the normal traffic patterns of our lives. When we become aware of our need to minister to people our first reaction is to "go out" and begin to hunt them. This is not really necessary. If we are sensitive, we will discover that people with needs are placed in the everyday context of our lives. But the clue to our discovering them lies within our concern and willingness to help.

When I was a young pastor I was still single. I enjoyed fellowship with the couples in the churches but was never too aware of any particular difficulties they had. Even after Barbara and I married I did not find myself doing too much counseling in this area. Then after we had been married a dozen years and were busy rearing our children, I found myself involved more and more with families who were having some sort of difficulty.

I commented about it to Barbara with the rather naive observation, "I wonder if people have been having these kinds of problems all along and I'm just now learning about them." Barbara was kind, but very penetrating, in her observation that perhaps the people were just beginning to pick up the signal from me that would indicate I would understand their problems and might be able to help. Since then I have had many occasions to observe that once a person is able and willing to help people he does not have to look for people to help. They are all around.

One of the deadly deterrents for Christians is the false picture often created that Christians do not have problems. The difference between a believer and an unbeliever is not that one has no problems and the other does. The difference is that the Christian is finding help in Christ and the church. Once an individual begins to let his humanity show, he increases the possibility of helping persons with both the ordinary problems of life and with the ultimate questions.

The world is so large and there are so many people that

a person makes a giant step when he learns to define the areas in which he has some responsibility. The inability to do this is what discourages so many people about the Great Commission (Matt. 28:18-20). "All the world" seems so impossible. I've discovered that to personalize the commission so it reads, "all *my* worlds," is of great help. This gives me a handle I can get hold of. This defines some areas in which I can assume responsibility. This allows me a basis of judging how I'm doing. Every individual has many worlds. The world of neighborhood. The world of work or school. The world of family and relatives. The world of social activities. The world of casual contact. If we will seek to love the individuals we come into contact with and see their many needs through the eyes of our Lord, then a ministry that bears witness to God's love will be both natural and effective. Not all of this will create an opportunity for a verbal witness, but some of it will. Not all of it will result in people becoming Christians, but some of it will. For when we live before people the Christian life, we create a favorable climate in which the Holy Spirit can do his work best.

I think that Annie Johnson Flint's little three-stanza poem summarizes well the importance of the witnessing life:

> Christ has no hands but our hands
> To do His work today;
> He has no feet but our feet
> To lead men in His way;
> He has no tongue but our tongues
> To tell men how He died
> He has no help but our help
> To bring them to His side.
>
> We are the only Bible
> The careless world will read;
> We are the sinner's gospel,

We are the scoffer's creed;
We are the Lord's last message
    Given in deed and word—
What if the line is crooked?
    What if the type is blurred?

What if our hands are busy
    With other work than His?
What if our feet are walking
    Where sin's allurement is?
What if our tongues are speaking
    Of things His lips would spurn?
How can we hope to help Him
    Unless from him we learn?

10
GETTING THE WHOLE TEAM READY
Ephesians 4:11-16

For years God has been sending me messages about the laity, and some really sneaked up on me. For instance, there was the night I turned on the television just as Eric Sevareid, longtime correspondent for the Columbia Broadcasting System, was beginning an interview with Eric Hoffer, the longshoreman philosopher. My only previous awareness of Hoffer came from a review I'd read of one of his books. My first reaction was to the contrast between the two men. Sevaried, who is a rather distinguished looking gentleman to begin with, was dressed immaculately. Hoffer had no coat or tie, his collar was open, and he kept mopping his perspiring face with a wadded-up handkerchief.

There were many interesting insights in the hour-long interview, but the one that I remember the most came during a discussion of what it was like during the depression. Hoffer told of how so many of the longshoremen were out of work and desperate.

On a particular occasion the California Highway Department had come down to the docks to hire some men to build roads in the mountains. As Hoffer related it, they had no sophisticated personnel processing. They had a big truck and when the truck was filled the job was closed. When they arrived in the mountains, there was a minimum of supervision. The men sort of organized themselves by learning what each had to contribute out of his abilities and experiences. Then Hoffer concluded, "In the morning we got up and began to build the road." Then he added, almost as an afterthought, "And, if we hadn't already had a constitution we could have written that, too."

I sat there stunned by this man's marvelous confidence in the ordinary man's insight and ability. Suddenly I realized that nothing would be more helpful to the church than for those who exercise leadership to begin looking at the whole people of God and to be aware of the amazing potential they have. This is no new dream. This is what God has had in mind all along. We've just been slow coming to it.

The most insightful writing in the New Testament concerning the role of the laity was written by the apostle Paul in Ephesians 4:11-16. Though the past several decades have witnessed a steady stream of biblical scholars who have reminded us of the truth in this passage, I personally am indebted to my friend Elton Trueblood for recovering its intended meaning. The problem with the older translations is that they put a comma in the middle of verse twelve, making the "perfecting of the saints" and the "work of the ministry" two different works, both to be performed by the pastor-teacher. The true meaning is reflected in this translation: "And these were his gifts; some to be apostles, some prophets, some evangelists, some pastors and teachers, to equip God's people for work in his service, to the building up of the body of Christ" (Eph. 4:11-12). This makes clear that the purpose for which the people of God are to be equipped is *to do the work of ministry.* This brief passage lays the foundation for an almost revolutionary view of how the church is supposed to get its work done and how it is supposed to carry out the Great Commission.

Paul lists the offices almost in the order in which they appeared, their order of importance, and the order in which they disappeared. Today we have only two of the four groups mentioned.

The apostles were the "launch group" for the early church. They had to have seen Jesus Christ personally, to bear witness to the resurrection, and to have been appointed by Christ. The very restrictiveness of the requirements meant that they would only function in the first generation of the church.

The prophets got their authority not from having seen Jesus Christ or borne witness to the resurrection, but from the Holy Spirit. They went from church to church with a message of great power. Though they had no home and no income they did have, for a period of fifteen or twenty years, great authority. They eventually vanished for different reasons. First, when the persecution came they were the most visible and the most vulnerable. Second, with great power comes the temptation to abuse and there was some of this. Third, as the churches grew in size and maturity, local leadership developed which was able to give supervision to the work on a day-to-day basis, making the itinerant prophet less needed and really less helpful.

The evangelists were the people who went where there were no churches in order to share the gospel. The most contemporary analogy would be that of a missionary who crosses cultural and national barriers to share the gospel where it has not been heard.

The last group mentioned was pastors and teachers. This is really two different functions of one group. Theirs was an interesting and important responsibility. They were the repository for the gospel. With few written accounts and fewer who could read, the need for one who would safeguard the

gospel was essential. Their other function was that of shep-
herds—to feed the flock and defend it against enemies. They
were essentially there to equip people spiritually, intellectually, and in every other way to serve Jesus Christ and
do his work in the world.

The phrase translated *equip* is full of helpful pictures. It
has been used to describe the setting of a joint which has
been broken, the mending of a net which has been torn,
and the reconciliation of opposing political factions. Here
Paul very specifically spells out the goal. Even a cursory
reading of Ephesians 4:13-16 tells of the aim for unity, maturity, knowledge, stability, honesty, love, and discernment. As
pastor I am convinced that the pastor-teacher office is mine
and that the responsibilities which Paul describes are still
in effect. As I look at the wonderful people God has given
me to shepherd I am filled with awe as I think of the responsibility of being their equipper. But I know that the work
of God will not be done until the people of God have been
made ready.

The very first barrier to be faced is this—nearly everyone
underestimates the potential of the laity. This is not just a
problem for church leadership. It isn't really news that many
of us who are pastors underestimate the laity. But it did
surprise me a bit to discover that the average lay person
underestimates both himself and his peers.

It's so interesting to notice how hard it is to believe in
the abilities of the people we've known all along. Once,
several years ago, I was the victim of this particular prejudice.
It was the first time I had been asked to be the main speaker
for a week at my denomination's western assembly at
Glorieta, New Mexico.

A pastor from California brought a large group of his
members to the week. After getting them registered and

assigned to housing, he asked the registrar, "Who is the preacher for the week?" When he was told that I was the one he said, "I think I'll just pack up and go home." The registrar, with whom I had been friends since college, was a bit surprised at the response and asked if there were something about me that the pastor didn't like. To this he replied, "No. I like him. But we were graduated at the same time"— the inference being that he couldn't possibly have been in school with anyone who would have anything helpful to say. We are always underestimating our peers.

John Newport tells the delightful story of a man who stole a horse and was promptly caught. When the thief was being arraigned, the judge asked if he would prefer to be tried by a panel of judges or a jury of his peers. The fellow wasn't sure he understood so he asked the judge, "Just exactly what is a peer?" When he was told by the judge that a peer was someone like him, he quickly decided he wanted the panel of judges, since, as he put it, "I don't want to be tried by a bunch of horse thieves." A lot of us have a low view of our own potential and it reflects in how we feel about others.

Many pastors and their people would be amazed at the insight, ability, interest, commitment, and creativity which the people have. One of the reasons is that we so seldom give them a real opportunity to show what they can do. My learning really to trust others has been a slow and sometimes painful experience.

One of the big steps for me was learning to trust my students. Many classes in seminary are content and idea oriented. But evangelism classes have the potential of reaching outside the classroom in some practical activity. During a particular semester I was covered up with invitations to do speaking engagements and participate on programs relating to evangelism. Most of these invitations I was not going to be able to accept.

As I was preparing to write letters of regret to them, my wife asked if I had considered sending my students. I was shocked. And something of my amazement must have shown in the way I said, "My students?" The thought of some poor program chairman expecting a "professor" and ending up with several "students" must have shown in my face. Barbara said: "Look, they are all college graduates. Most of them are married and have families. In a couple of years they will be good leaders in the churches. Maybe you're underestimating your students' ability." I knew she was right so I decided to try.

I called those who had invited me and suggested the students. They liked the idea. Then I went into my classes, read the invitation, and asked who would be willing to get a group together, plan the program, and then present it. I "farmed out" all the invitations with these instructions. "Don't check with me. Meet and pray. Get in contact with the people and get all the details worked out. Then plan what you think you ought to do—and do it."

They took me at my word and it's a good thing, because I'd have been nervous if I had had any idea some of the things they would do. They wrote plays and songs, had panels and question-and-answer periods, gave testimonies, played all kinds of musical instruments, and once in a while *preached a sermon.* But the rewarding thing about the whole experience was that not one group let me down. And the evaluations which came in from those who had originally invited me was that these were the best programs they had ever had. The next year they invited my students instead of me! And already some of those young people who seemed to have so little potential as they sat alphabetically in *Evangelisn 101* are making their mark in the world.

In watching different lay persons relate to each other, I've seen this same prejudice I had toward my students at work. Often we refuse to let people grow up. In spite of the fact that they have graduated from college, gotten married, and are working in some responsible position in a corporation, there are always people who will say: "Isn't that Ben's boy? I used to have him in the first grade class." Our fear of growing older makes it hard to admit that some of the children we worked with are now adults.

Often we find it hard to believe that people can change and that maturing takes place. Seldom do I see someone given a demanding responsibility in the church but that at least one person comes around with, "Pastor, you haven't been here too long and I guess that there's really no way of your knowing. . . ." Then they tell me of some minor incident that took place twenty years ago in this person's life which they are sure would make it impossible for him to function in this particular job. We all need to learn to update and reevaluate one another. We need to put into practical use our belief in forgiveness and starting over, growth and maturity, and the potential of all of God's children.

Another real surprise to me has been the number of people who consistently underestimate themselves. It is true that the Bible has a lot to say about thinking more highly of ourselves than we ought. But sometimes I wish there were a verse or two urging people not to underestimate their own potential.

For years I was a member of an editorial advisory board of a publishing company and as such received copies of all the books they published. One time I was sent a book in which page 67 was blank. The pages before and after were printed, but this one page for some unknown reason was completely blank. I was telling a friend about this and to my utter surprise he said, "I identify with that blank page." I began checking around and was amazed at the number of people who felt that when God printed all the people there had been some sort of snafu and they were the result— page 67. All God's people need to hear again and again Paul's wonderful affirmation of our potential which he wrote to his friends in Corinth:

> There are varieties of gifts, but the same Spirit. There are varieties of service, but the same Lord. There are many forms of work, but all of them, in all men, are the work of the same God. In each of us the Spirit is manifested in one particular way, for some useful purpose (1 Cor. 12:4-7).

We also need a broader understanding of the group we're talking about when we speak of *laity*. Too many people get their definition from underlining the last three letters of "lay*men*." I've seen a number of men go to a "lay conference" and be surprised to find women there. Technically, laity means "the people of God."

It is not only a mistake to think of laity as men only, it is terrible to think of laity only as older adults. While I directed the work of evangelism for my denomination, we developed a program for training the lay persons in the sharing of their faith. Early in the planning stage the question was asked, "How old do you have to be to be a layman?" The answers reflected the ingrained prejudice which the church has against youth.

But the more we discussed the needs of the whole world for an effective witness and the new excitement among young people in the church, the more we realized that any definition of laity which omitted this group was inadequate. We included, as adults, in the training program high school freshmen and above. All the men and women and youth were put together both for the training and for the practical experience. It was one of the best ideas we had. Out of it came the conviction that the lay group in the church with the most potential in evangelism may be called "youth choir." We also came to the feeling that it was too patronizing to limit the participation of youth to "playing church" during an annual "youth week." Some way to make them a vital part of the church's ministry and witness must be found. We have too long limited ourselves in the church by looking to a handful of the "elite" for the work. The whole people of God need to be discovered.

There was a time when I limited "equipping" in my mind to special training in skills and techniques. Today I watch our people live their lives in the pressure of an increasingly secular world. I watch them trying to cope at work and play and in the rearing of their children. I'm a little more sympathetic with the larger needs they have as Christians. I'm also more aware of the great resource within the church for equipping the laity.

I have no permanent quarrel with the renewal movement as such. Friendships with Howard Butt, Keith Miller, Ben Johnson, Elton Trueblood, Bruce Larson, and others have made me a part of it. But I've come to see its only validity comes as it undergirds the church in its equipping ministry. Early thoughts of some viable alternative to the church have all been dropped as totally unrealistic.

The church has in its Bible study, fellowship, and worship the greatest possible tools for undergirding and equipping God's people. The Bible study organization in the church is essentially a lay organization. Although in a minority of the congregations there are staff members who are specialists in Christian education, most Sunday schools are led by laymen and manned by laymen. In the light of the importance of meaningful Bible study for Christian growth it is impera-

tive that the downward trend in enrollment and attendance
be reversed. The trend does not so much reflect a lack of
interest among adults in the Bible. Rather it suggests that
the church has done the seemingly impossible—it has taken
the most revolutionary and life-changing book ever written
and made its study boring. But this is not the case everywhere
and it does not have to be the situation anywhere.

I try to be a responsible teacher of the Scriptures from
the pulpit and in the midweek Bible study. But the most
significant teaching will be done in Sunday School departments where there are choices, where adults are treated as
adults, where trained teachers commit themselves to digging
the treasures from the Word of God and applying them to
the lives of their members.

The worship services have amazing potential for undergirding the people of God. The old adage, "people *ought*
to attend church," could well be changed to "people *need*
to attend church." The admonition that Christians are not
to forsake the assembling of themselves together was for their
own good. So many elements of the Christian life and our
own needs are involved. There is celebration, fellowship,
study and learning, prayer and Bible reading, meditation,
confession and forgiveness, and decision. The decisions which
are demanded in life, the temptations that come, the disappointments we suffer, the needs we come up against for which
we are not adequate, and the decisions we are called upon
to make for which we need wisdom make genuine worship
so necessary.

But unfortunately there can be a difference in "going to
church" and being in a worship service that strengthens. The
very ingredients which are so needed can also be elusive.
This leads to all sorts of efforts to make things "worshipful."
Worship will always reflect certain cultural tastes. There is

really nothing so bad about this. But true worship should have a certain joy and expectancy in it. It should have a believable quality as it translates the everlasting gospel into the lives which are to be lived this week. Worship, which is usually led by the professional staff, has tended to be too slow in making the changes that are needed. Nothing makes sharing life easier for a church member than sensing Christ's presence in a fresh and challenging way each week. Nothing makes it easier in sharing his faith than being able to bring a friend, knowing the love and warmth and joy he will be able to sense. A church which is incapable of exciting worship will find effective evangelism almost impossible.

We have also tended to underestimate the average lay person's need for some specific training in the sharing of his faith. This is an area in which I have had to "eat crow." For years I believed that any person who was a Christian could use the skills he already had to witness. I was wrong.

I watched women who had drive and ingenuity enough to make them excellent presidents of the PTA who were unable to tell the children in their class how to become Christians. I watched lawyers who were qualified to try cases before the Supreme Court who could not sit down in the living room of an interested friend and present a good "brief" for Jesus Christ. While there are certain carryovers that relate to insights and attitudes, I've discovered that most of the best people in the church need some help in learning to communicate their faith. This is a help which the pastor should lead in providing. A failure to do this creates a vacuum which forces the interested Christian to go outside his own church to get help in what should be a primary task for the church. This is neither wise nor necessary. Just as every Christian can be taught better to share his faith, every pastor can learn to train the laymen.

There are a host of programs and adaptations of programs which are available. Many of the approaches developed by the interdenominational groups have been very helpful. The two approaches with which I'm most familiar, that are specifically geared to the local congregation and provide both a style of training lay persons and an ongoing program, are "Evangelism Explosion" which was developed at the Coral Ridge Presbyterian Church in Ft. Lauderdale, Florida, and the "Witness Involvement Now" (WIN) program which was developed by the evangelism staff of the Southern Baptist Convention. While these two approaches had their origin within certain denominations, they have both been adapted to other cultures, national groups, and to other denominations. It's rather interesting that at a time when most of the denominations have quit growing, Southern Baptists had their best year in the history of the group during the second year of an emphasis on training the laity. The churches today which are reaching large numbers of people for Jesus Christ are those who train their laity.

There are really explosive potentials involved when people begin to talk seriously about mobilizing the total resources of the church for sharing Christ. But it is not yet a movement. It is more like a "small cloud on the horizon."

I was once in a convention with Bill Pinson. We were on a panel together, discussing the overall condition of the church today. Bill had just spent a sabbatic leave studying all of the current movements in American society. He read their literature, attended their meetings, got acquainted with their leaders, and analyzed the overall aims and directions of the various groups. Since he had just finished writing up the report of his rather extensive study I asked him briefly to summarize some of the common characteristics of a movement. He listed four: (1) they all have a charismatic leader;

(2) they know what they believe and are able to communicate it with people in terms they can understand; (3) they are willing to sacrifice for their cause; and (4) they really believe in their hearts that they are going to change the world.

We all listened to his appraisal. Then I gestured to the audience with my hand and asked of Bill, "Do you think they represent a movement by the terms you've just described?" I'm sure that everyone expected a quick yes. But he just sat there quietly for what seemed like an eternity and then sadly shook his head and said: "No, this is not a movement. They don't have that look in their eye. You can tell by the way they sit and listen, and by listening to them talk, they're not a movement." Then, as everyone was trying to recover from the shock and from the obvious accuracy of his answer, he continued, "But it's not because God doesn't want them to be."

As I have looked with great encouragement at the new interest in the laity and the new enthusiasm among the laity I wonder if it is really a movement. And in all honesty I have to answer, "No, not yet. But it isn't because God doesn't want it to be." God's plan, from the beginning, has been to involve the whole people of God in sharing the gospel. The new excitement about the laity is a "small cloud on the horizon." My prayer is that the last fourth of the twentieth century will see an outpouring of training and sharing. I've made a committment to that end. Don't be reluctant. Join me.